Collins Nature Guide

BUTTERFLIES AND MOTHS
OF BRITAIN & EUROPE
H. Hofmann • T. Marktanner

Translated by
ADRIAN PONT
Scientific Consultant David Carter

D0039423

HarperCollins*Publishers*

Introduction

With their gorgeous shapes and colours, butterflies and moths are amongst the most distinctive creatures in the natural world. The beauty and delicacy of their wings, the variety of their colours, their amazing metamorphosis and their astonishing abilities never cease to fascinate and amaze. Even caterpillars, which appear so insignificant at first sight, display an unexpected variety in form and colour when studied more closely.

The handy format of *Collins Nature Guide to Butterflies and Moths* makes it ideal for anyone who wishes to get to know butterflies and moths, or wishes to identify what they see at home or abroad. The butterflies of Europe and the most important moths are covered with 245 superb colour photographs, 50 colour drawings illustrating their biology, caterpillars and typical food plants, and detailed descriptions. In many cases where the two sexes have a strikingly different appearance or where the uppersides and undersides of the wings have a different pattern, this is illustrated with a second picture, either on the page with the illustrations (right-hand page) or within the text (at the bottom of the left-hand page). The text provides basic information on the most important characteristics, geographic distribution, habitat preferences, flight-period and habits for each species, as well as behaviour, food plants and pupation sites for the caterpillars, and the type of hibernation each one undertakes.

The section *Introduction to butterflies and moths* (p. 148) highlights interesting aspects of butterfly biology, structure, sense perception, survival strategies and reproduction. Also explained is the way of life of the caterpillars and their miraculous transformation into adult butterflies and moths. The pictures on the inside of the back cover give examples of how perfectly the adults, caterpillars and chrysalises can camouflage themselves. The section *Threats and conservation* (p. 154) explains why the numbers of these colourful inhabitants of our countryside are sinking lower and lower, and what each one of us can do to further the preservation and conservation of our butterflies and moths. The *Index* (p. 156) lists all the species discussed in this book under both their English and scientific names.

The following abbreviations are used in the text:

⚐ = species occurring in the British Isles
(⚐) = species occurring in the British Isles, but a rare or vagrant species
♂ = male
♀ = female

All altitudes given are measured in metres (m) above sea level.

Colour	Butterfly group	Page number
	YELLOW includes the Swallowtails, Whites and Yellows (families Papilionidae and Pieridae)	8–25
	RED includes the Aristocrats and Fritillaries (family Nymphalidae)	26–55
	GREEN includes the so-called Browns (family Satyridae)	56–79
	BLUE includes the Hairstreaks, Coppers and Blues (family Lycaenidae)	80–101
	BROWN includes the Skippers (family Hesperiidae)	102–111
	GREY covers all the Moths, from a variety of families (e.g. Arctiidae, Geometridae, Lasiocampidae, Lymantriidae, Noctuidae, Saturniidae, Sphingidae, Zygaenidae)	112–145

The authors:
Dr Helga Hofmann is a biologist who works at the Ludwig-Maximilian University in Munich, Germany. She is the author of numerous natural history books, including *Collins Nature Guide to Wild Animals*.
Thomas Marktanner has been a nature photographer and student of the butterflies and moths for 30 years. He is particularly involved in faunistic studies and conservation.

From egg to butterfly...

1 An egg batch

2 Caterpillars hatching

3 Colony of young caterpillars

The stages through which a butterfly or moth must pass before it is a fully fledged adult ready to fly through the air are shown here, using the Peacock butterfly as an example.

A batch of eggs is laid by the female butterfly on the underside of a Stinging-nettle leaf (1).

After some two weeks the tiny caterpillars hatch (2). They do not eat their eggshells but make their way to the tender young terminal shoots of their food plant, where they spin a protective web of silk. They remain together in their communal web which they only leave for feeding (3).

Thanks to their voracious appetite, the caterpillars grow rapidly and have to moult as their skins become too tight. As they feed and grow they move in a group from one nettle to another.

After the last moult (4) the caterpillars dispense with their protective web and disperse. Each one attaches itself by the hind end to the stem or leaf of a plant. The skin splits open at the neck, and the chrysalis, which is soft and mobile at this stage, twists and struggles to free itself (5, 6).

4 Caterpillars after the final moult

5 Caterpillar preparing to pupate

...the miraculous transformation

11 Ready to fly off

10 Adult on the empty chrysalis case

Eventually the larval skin is pushed into a ball at the tail-end of the chrysalis, and the outer chitinous sheath gradually hardens (7).
Within this pupal case the fundamental change takes place, from 'eating machine' caterpillar to winged adult.
This is usually completed within 14-18 days, after which the adult butterfly bursts the chrysalis and wriggles out (8, 9).
Still wet and with limp, crumpled wings, the butterfly hangs for a while from the empty chrysalis (10).
As blood and oxygen are pumped through the wing veins, the wings expand (11).
This takes about ten minutes, and a few hours later the wings have hardened sufficiently for the butterfly to take its first flight.

9 The adult emerges

8 The emergence process begins

6 A final moult reveals the chrysalis

7 Chrysalis (pupa)

1   Swallowtail 🦋   *Papilio machaon*

(Swallowtails)

Description: Wingspan 6-8 cm. With a vivid yellow and black pattern, hind wing with a blue dusted band and an orange to red-brown eye-spot; hind wing produced into a tail-like projection, from which the butterfly takes its name.

Distribution: Throughout Europe (in British Isles confined to the wetlands of eastern England), from coasts up to 2000 m; mainly in unimproved flower-rich meadows and rough areas, also in gardens.

Flight period: Early Apr to Oct; two or three broods, but only one at higher ·altitudes.

Behaviour: A powerful flyer, which can cover large distances; visits flowers to feed on nectar; ♂ often aggregate around hilltops and await the arrival of ♀ for mating; eggs laid singly on the stems, leaves and pedicels (flower stalks) of the caterpillar's food plants.

Caterpillar: Black with a white 'saddle' and red warts at first, later becoming greenish with black rings and orange dots, without hairs; when danger threatens, a pair of 'horns' is extruded from the neck area, which give off an unpleasant odour. Feeds singly and by day on Wild Carrot, Milk Parsley, Fennel and other umbels. Chrysalis green or brown, attached by a girdle to a plant stem.

Hibernation: As a chrysalis on a plant stem, often away from the food plant.

Note: The subspecies found in Britain, ssp. *britannicus*, is confined to the fenlands of eastern England.

2   Scarce Swallowtail   *Iphiclides podalirius*

(Swallowtails)

Description: Wingspan 6-7.5 cm, ♀ rather larger than ♂. Similar to the Swallowtail, but ground-colour paler yellowish to almost white, the black pattern consisting of black bands of varying length, hind wing with distinctly longer 'tails', eye-spots black-blue with an orange crescent above.

Distribution: Southern Europe, north of the Alps only in especially mild areas, in mountains up to 1600 m; favours rocky but flower-rich habitats with shrubby vegetation.

Flight period: Early Apr to late Aug; one or two broods.

Behaviour: Ranges widely and visits flowers to feed on nectar; commonly uses thermal upcurrents for soaring. When ready to mate, ♂ assemble around hilltops and await ♀; eggs laid singly on the upper- and undersides of leaves.

Caterpillar: Unusually stout, green with reddish spots, a yellow stripe on the back, and diagonal stripes on sides; difficult to find. When disturbed, it extrudes a pair of yellow 'horns' from the neck area which give off an unpleasant odour. Feeds singly on Sloe, but also on hawthorn, St. Lucie Cherry, Snowy Mespil and certain fruit trees. Chrysalis attached by a girdle to a twig of the host tree.

Hibernation: As a chrysalis; the overwintering chrysalis is brown, whilst that of the summer brood is green.

Southern Festoon

Zerynthia polyxena

(Swallowtails)

Description: Wingspan 4.5-5.5 cm. Ground-colour pale yellow with a vivid black and red pattern, but forewing without red markings or with only small red spots.

Distribution: South of the Alps, in Lower Austria, Hungary and countries of the eastern Mediterranean; on dry, sunny slopes up to about 800 m.

Flight period: Early Apr to late May; one brood.

Behaviour: Warmth-loving, and usually flying only when the sun shines; visits flowers. Eggs laid singly or in groups on blossoms or the underside of leaves of the caterpillar's food plant.

Caterpillar: Reddish yellow or grey, with numerous red-brown spines that are black tipped and covered with bristly hairs. Lives and feeds on species of birthwort; absorbs the poisons of the plants so that both caterpillar and adult are unpalatable to birds and other enemies. Chrysalis long, slender, grey, attached by a girdle.

Hibernation: As a chrysalis, not infrequently through two winters.

Note: Not found in the Iberian Peninsula, where it is replaced by the Spanish Festoon (*Z. rumina*) which is similar but has an extensive pattern of red spots on forewing.

Apollo

Parnassius apollo

(Swallowtails)

Description: Wingspan 6.5-8 cm. Wings whitish, more or less transparent around edges, with black spots; hind wing with red or orange eye-spots, which are ringed with black and usually have white centres. Abdomen of ♂ (picture) densely haired, of ♀ sparsely haired or bare.

Distribution: Mountainous areas throughout Europe, to over 2000 m; mainly in rocky meadows and steppes and on stony slopes, especially in limestone regions.

Flight period: Early May to late Sep; one brood.

Behaviour: With a slow and floating flight, sometimes soars; visits flowers to feed (prefers violets and thistles), often spending the night there; ♂ commonly patrols along slopes while searching for a mate; ♀ attaches eggs singly to the caterpillar's food plant, or to stones, twigs or dry grasses in the immediate vicinity.

Caterpillar: Black, with small steel-blue warts and rows of orange-red spots, with short hairs. Only feeds when the sun is out, on White Stonecrop and Orpine; gregarious when young, but living singly later on. Forms a stout, bluish-white dusted chrysalis, which rests on the ground in a delicate cocoon.

Hibernation: Usually as an egg, in which the caterpillar is fully formed; many hatch in autumn and overwinter as young caterpillars.

Note: Numerous local races have been recognised which differ from each other in the grey or yellowish shades of the ground-colour and in the size and colour of the eye-spots.

1 | # Small Apollo | *Parnassius phoebus*

(Swallowtails)

Description: Wingspan 6-7 cm. Very similar to the Apollo (see p. 10), the ♂ usually rather more yellow, the ♀ (picture) with ground-colour more grey, usually with small red eye-spots on forewing too.

Distribution: Only in the Alps, between 1500 m and 2600 m; close to streams and boggy areas.

Flight period: Late June to early Sep; one brood.

Behaviour: Similar to that of the Apollo; ♂ flies in the morning up and down streams, restlessly searching for a ♀ that is ready to mate; ♀ lays eggs singly on the caterpillar's food plant or on stones, dry twigs etc., in the immediate vicinity, or simply drops them to the ground.

Caterpillar: Black, with short hairs that are situated on small warts, with rows of orange- to lemon-yellow spots. Feeds only on Yellow Saxifrage. Chrysalis brown, flattened, in a loose cocoon on the ground, often beneath stones.

Hibernation: As an egg, in which the caterpillar is fully formed, more rarely as a young caterpillar.

2 | # Clouded Apollo | *Parnassius mnemosyne*

(Swallowtails)

Description: Wingspan 5.2-6 cm. Unlike the other Apollo species, has black spots but no red ones.

Distribution: Throughout Europe except for the Iberian Peninsula, British Isles and northern Scandinavia; in moist grassy habitats, the herb-rich edges of deciduous woods, and in forest meadows, at altitudes of 500 m to over 1600 m. With only a few additional isolated records.

Flight period: Mid-May to mid-Aug; one brood.

Behaviour: Flight rapid; when disturbed, it simply drops down into the grass; ♂ flies restlessly around until early afternoon, searching for ♀, and only then feeds on flowers; ♀ lays eggs on stones, wood or dry grasses in areas where corydalis, the caterpillar's food plant, grows.

Caterpillar: Black, with short hairs, with longitudinal rows of yellow to orange spots on sides. Lives on various species of corydalis, feeding only during fine weather and hiding under leaves or stones at other times. Chrysalis clay-yellow, in a loose cocoon on the ground.

Hibernation: As an egg, in which the caterpillar is fully formed; occasionally as a newly-hatched caterpillar.

Note: There are numerous local races and forms, which differ mainly in the intensity of the white or grey wing-scales.

The caterpillar of the Clouded Apollo lives only on corydalis.

1 Wood White ⚥

Leptidea sinapis

(Whites and Yellows)

Description: Wingspan 3.5-4.2 cm. ♂ almost pure white, ♀ with a grey to black spot at tip of forewing upperside (picture: ♂ and ♀).

Distribution: Almost throughout Europe (except Scotland and northern Scandinavia), up to 2000 m; prefers the edges of woods, clearings, water meadows and parks.

Flight period: Early Apr to late Oct; two or three broods, but only one at higher altitudes (July or Aug).

Behaviour: With a slow fluttering flight; visits flowers; eggs laid singly on the underside of leaves of the caterpillar's food plants.

Caterpillar: Green with narrow yellow stripes along the sides, with short hairs. Feeds especially on Meadow Vetchling, but also on Slender Vetch, Crown Vetch, Birds-foot Trefoil and other plants. Chrysalis attached by a girdle to the stem of the food plant, resembling a dead leaf.

Hibernation: As a chrysalis.

2 Brimstone ⚥

Gonepteryx rhamni

(Whites and Yellows)

Description: Wingspan 5-6 cm. Each wing with a small pointed tip; ♂ (picture) intensely lemon-yellow, ♀ yellowish- to greenish-white (and sometimes confused in flight with the Large White, p. 18), with a small orange dot at middle of each wing. Always rests with wings closed.

Distribution: Throughout Europe except for northern Ireland, Scotland and northern Scandinavia, in mountains to over 2000 m; common in forests and adjacent areas, but also in areas of scrub, parks and gardens.

Flight period: Early July to Oct, and, after overwintering as an adult, from Feb or Mar to June, in one brood; inactive during the hottest weeks of summer.

Behaviour: One of the first butterflies to appear in spring; feeds at flowers on nectar. The ♂ patrols with great tenacity along woodland margins or clearings whilst searching for ♀. During the courtship dance, the ♀ flies first and the ♂ follows at a fixed distance, as if attached by an invisible thread. With mating and egg-laying, which usually take place in April, the life-cycle of the butterfly is completed.

Caterpillar: Green, with whitish stripes along sides, without hairs. Feeds on various buckthorn species; it forms a small cushion of silk close to the midrib of the leaf on which it is living and feeding. Chrysalis strikingly angular, green, with pale yellow stripes down the sides, attached to the stem of the food plant by a girdle.

Hibernation: As an adult butterfly, usually choosing an evergreen plant for this (it is the only central European butterfly that hibernates without seeking out a more protected site).

Note: With a life-span of 10-11 months, this is the longest lived of all our indigenous butterflies.

Pale Clouded Yellow (♀) *Colias hyale*

(Whites and Yellows)

Description: Wingspan 4.4-5 cm. ♂ (picture) pale yellow, ♀ whitish yellow, both with a diffuse blackish marginal band and a black central spot on upperside of forewing, underside of hind wing with two small contiguous circles that form a figure 8.

Distribution: Central and eastern Europe, sometimes migrating to central Scandinavia and a rare visitor to Britain; in mountains up to 2000 m; in open countryside, common in pastures and clover fields.

Flight period: Early May to late Oct; two or three broods, but only one at higher altitudes.

Behaviour: A very active flyer, visiting flowers to feed on nectar; eggs laid singly on the upperside of leaves of the caterpillar's food plant; whitish at first, becoming red-brown later.

Caterpillar: Green, with small, fine, black spots, with a yellowish or reddish longitudinal line on each side. Feeds mainly on Lucerne, but also on other species of clover and related plants. Chrysalis green and attached by a girdle.

Hibernation: As a caterpillar.

Clouded Yellow ♀ *Colias crocea*

(Whites and Yellows)

Description: Wingspan 4.5-5.2 cm. Uppersides of wings orange-yellow to deep orange, undersides yellow; unlike the ♂ (picture), the ♀ has yellow spots in the black marginal band. Whitish ♀ sometimes occur.

Distribution: In the warmer regions of Europe, especially the lowlands, only rarely above 1600 m; migrates as far as England and Scandinavia in many summers; in open, dry countryside.

Flight period: Early Apr to early Nov; probably two or three broods.

Behaviour: A rapid flyer which migrates northwards over large distances; feeds on nectar-rich flowers; ♀ lays eggs singly on the upperside of leaves of the caterpillar's food plants.

Caterpillar: Dark green, with yellow lines on sides that are patterned with black dots and red streaks. Feeds mainly on Lucerne but also on other related plants. Chrysalis green, attached by a girdle.

Hibernation: As a caterpillar, but only in frost-free regions; the northern parts of its range are recolonised every year by butterflies that migrate from the south.

Similar species: The Moorland Clouded Yellow (*Colias palaeno*, picture 3) is found in central and northern Europe in flower-rich areas on the edge of high moors and in dwarf-shrub heaths in mountains up to 2500 m. It flies from early May to late Oct; the dark green caterpillar, with shining yellow side stripes, feeds on Crowberry.

1   # Large White 🜬   *Pieris brassicae*

(Whites and Yellows)

Description: Wingspan 5.3-6.5 cm. Forewing with a black tip, in ♀ (small picture) with two further black spots, undersides yellowish.
Distribution: Throughout Europe, in the mountains up to 2000 m; prefers open areas, and closely associated with agriculture, in gardens and parks, meadows and fields; common everywhere.
Flight period: Early Apr to Oct; two or three broods.
Behaviour: Mating flight spiralling and vivacious; copulating pairs often remain joined for a long time, and when disturbed fly off still linked together; ♀ lays golden-yellow eggs in batches close together on the underside of leaves of the caterpillar's food plants.
Caterpillar: Yellowish green, with black spots of various sizes and yellow lines on the top and sides, with short hairs. Feeds mainly on various cabbage species (this butterfly is also known as the Cabbage White), but also on Nasturtium, Hedge-mustard and other plants which are frequently reduced to a skeleton. The young caterpillars remain together at first, but disperse later. Chrysalis yellow-green with a pattern of black spots, attached by a girdle on or near the food plant.
Hibernation: As a chrysalis, commonly on buildings, crevices in walls, under window ledges, etc.

2   # Small White 🜬   *Pieris rapae*

(Whites and Yellows)

Description: Wingspan 4-5.2 cm. Very similar to the Large White except for its smaller size; ♂ (picture) with one dark spot on forewing, which varies greatly in intensity.
Distribution: Throughout Europe up to 2000 m, common everywhere, sometimes in great numbers.
Flight period: Mid-Mar to Oct; two to four broods.
Behaviour: Similar to that of the Large White. Eggs generally laid singly on the underside of leaves of the caterpillar's food plant.
Caterpillar: Light green with a fine yellow line along the back, with short hairs. First brood caterpillars solitary, feeding on Rape, Hedge-mustard, Charlock and other plants, second brood feeds mainly on species of cabbage, preferring the heart to the outer leaves. Chrysalis attached by a girdle on or close to the food plant.
Hibernation: As a chrysalis.
Note: One of the most abundant butterflies anywhere.

The ♀ of the Large White has black spots on the forewing.

Green-veined White ⚐ *Pieris napi*

1

(Whites and Yellows)

Description: Wingspan 4-4.6 cm. (Picture: ♀.) Very similar to the Small
White (see p. 18), veins on underside of wings dark dusted. There are
seasonal differences in size and colour: the spring brood is smaller, and
with a darker and more distinct pattern.

Distribution: Throughout Europe, to an altitude of 2000 m; common
everywhere, preferring cool damp places, meadows, shrubby slopes and the
edges of deciduous woods.

Flight period: Mid-Mar to Oct; two or three broods, but only one at higher
altitudes.

Behaviour: An active butterfly with a zigzag flight; commonly feeds at
flowers on nectar, especially on thistles; ♀ lays greenish spindle-shaped
eggs singly or in small batches on the underside of leaves of the caterpillar's
food plant.

Caterpillar: Slender, green, with small black-haired warts, breathing
openings (spiracles) black and surrounded by yellow. Feeds on
Cuckooflower and related species such as Watercress, Hedge-mustard,
Garlic Mustard, Charlock and other crucifers. Chrysalis yellowish green
and black-spotted, attached by a girdle to plant stems.

Hibernation: As a chrysalis. Unlike the summer chrysalis, the overwintering
chrysalis is whitish and with almost no pattern.

Dark-veined White *Pieris bryoniae*

2/3

(Whites and Yellows)

Description: Wingspan 4.2-4.7 cm. The ♂ (picture 2) is similar to the
Green-veined White (some specialists consider it to be a subspecies),
♀ (picture 3) usually strongly yellowish grey with broad, dark grey veins.

Distribution: Isolated localities in European mountains between 800 m and
2000 m, and in Scandinavia; in alpine meadows, in the north also on heaths.

Flight period: Early May to late Aug; one or two broods.

Behaviour: Visits flowers to feed on nectar; the greenish eggs are laid singly
on the caterpillar's food plant.

Caterpillar: Slender, matt green, with small black-haired warts. Feeds on
Buckler Mustard, Cuckooflower and other alpine crucifers. Chrysalis pale
green, attached by a girdle to plant stems; wing-sheaths becoming
conspicuously red before the adult butterfly emerges.

Hibernation: As a chrysalis.

Note: Because of its patchy distribution, the Dark-veined White has broken
up into many geographical races and numerous individual forms.

1 Black-veined White · *Aporia crataegi*

(Whites and Yellows)

Description: Wingspan 6-7 cm. Wings white, almost transparent, with strikingly black veins. Rustles noticeably in flight.

Distribution: Throughout Europe except for northern Scandinavia and British Isles, in mountains to over 1600 m; in open countryside, orchards and water meadows. Can occur locally in enormous numbers, and then be completely absent for years.

Flight period: Mid-May to late July; one brood.

Behaviour: A strong and elegant flyer; visits flowers to feed on nectar; ♂ performs a strikingly fluttering mating flight; ♀ lays eggs in dense batches on the upperside of leaves of the caterpillar's food plant.

Caterpillar: Ash-grey, with black and orange longitudinal stripes, with dense hairs. Feeds on hawthorn species, Sloe, Rowan, fruit trees, and other deciduous trees. Chrysalis yellow with black spots, attached by a girdle.

Hibernation: As young caterpillars in a communal web spun between the leaves of the food plant.

Note: Mass occurrences, which often led to the Black-veined White becoming an orchard pest, have now become very rare. Became extinct in the British Isles in the 1920s.

2 Bath White (🗷) · *Pontia daplidice*

(Whites and Yellows)

Description: Wingspan 3.5-4.8 cm. Wings white, uppersides with brown to black spots which are darker and larger in ♀ (picture); hind wing with olive-green spots on underside.

Distribution: Central and southern Europe, a rare visitor to Britain, almost to 2000 m, varying in abundance north of the Alps and generally restricted to limited areas; prefers sunny, dry, often rough stony or sandy areas.

Flight period: Early Apr to mid-Oct; two or three generations.

Behaviour: With a rapid zigzag flight, usually low over the ground; migrates large distances northwards in favourable years; eggs laid singly on the leaves and flowers of the caterpillar's host plants.

Caterpillar: Grey-green with small dot-like black warts and four longitudinal yellow lines. Feeds on mignonette species, White Mustard and other crucifers; chrysalis attached by a girdle to the food plant.

Hibernation: As a chrysalis.

The caterpillar of the Black-veined White feeds on hawthorn.

Orange Tip ⌇
(Whites and Yellows)

Anthocharis cardamines

Description: Wingspan 3.5-4.5 cm. Ground-colour white, tip of forewing grey, in ♂ outer half of forewing shining orange (right picture), ♀ with no orange colour (small picture), hind wing with underside dappled greenish in both sexes.

Distribution: Throughout Europe (except southern Spain and Scandinavia), up to 2000 m; especially in open woodlands, along edges of woods, and in damp flower-rich meadows.

Flight period: Late Mar to late July; one brood.

Behaviour: An eager flower visitor; rests with the wings closed, and the dappled underside provides good camouflage; ♀ ready to mate as soon as she hatches from the chrysalis, and rests on the ground with half-open wings whilst awaiting a ♂; eggs laid singly on stems and flower-buds of the caterpillar's food plants.

Caterpillar: Blue-green with small black dots and broad white side stripes. Feeds on Cuckooflower, Garlic Mustard, Tower Mustard and other crucifers, consuming flowers and seed capsules; the fully grown caterpillar leaves the food plant and forms a narrow, curved, green or brownish chrysalis attached by a girdle to another plant stem in the vicinity.

Hibernation: As a chrysalis, sometimes through two winters.

Southern Orange Tip
(Whites and Yellows)

Anthocharis euphenoides

Description: Wingspan 3.2-3.8 cm. The ♂ (picture) intensely yellow in ground-colour with tip of forewing orange-red, ♀ yellowish white with wing-tip brownish orange.

Distribution: Southwest Europe and the valleys of the southern Alps, up to 2000 m.

Flight period: Early Apr to late June; one brood.

Behaviour: Visits flowers, commonly those of mustard species; otherwise similar to that of the Orange Tip.

Caterpillar: Greenish with distinct black dots, white side stripes, and a yellow and black pattern on the back. Feeds exclusively on Buckler Mustard; chrysalis green, brown or grey, strongly curved, attached by a girdle.

Hibernation: As a chrysalis.

The ♀ Orange Tip lacks the striking orange of the ♂.

Poplar Admiral

Limenitis populi

(Aristocrats)

Description: Wingspan 6.5-8 cm, ♀ larger than ♂ (picture 1). Upperside dark brown with white, orange and black spots, the white more extensive in ♀; underside (picture 2) with a vivid orange-brown and grey-blue pattern.

Distribution: Northern and central Europe and far to the east (but absent from western Europe and the British Isles), in the Alps up to 1500 m; in damp, open deciduous woods; not common anywhere.

Flight period: Late May to early Aug; one brood.

Behaviour: Flies mainly at treetop level, coming to the ground only for water and food; feeds on wet soil, animal excrement and carrion; ♂ commonly rests on particular branches with the wings outspread, waiting for a passing ♀; competing males are driven off with violent attacks; ♀ lays eggs singly on the upperside of leaves of the caterpillar's food plant, usually right on the leaf-tips.

Caterpillar: Green, on each side with a light irregular band, a pattern of black shadows; two rows of spines on the back, of which the front pair is the longest. Feeds on Aspen and other species of poplar. Chrysalis hangs suspended from a leaf on a silk pad.

Hibernation: As a young caterpillar, singly or in small groups within a rolled-up leaf at the tip of a twig.

White Admiral 🔲

Limenitis camilla

(Aristocrats)

Description: Wingspan 5-6 cm. Upperside black-brown with a white band, underside with the same colourful pattern as the Poplar Admiral but the colours not so intense.

Distribution: Range more or less as the Poplar Admiral, but also occurs in England; in damp water meadows and open woodlands, along forest rides and clearings.

Flight period: Mid-June to mid-Aug, one brood; in the south sometimes from May to Sep, with two broods.

Behaviour: Does not generally fly high above the ground, also visits flowers; otherwise similar to the Poplar Admiral.

Caterpillar: Green with purple-red underside, with two rows of spines of varying lengths on the back. Feeds on Fly Honeysuckle and other honeysuckles; forms a whitish-grey suspended chrysalis.

Hibernation: As a caterpillar, like the Poplar Admiral.

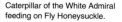

Caterpillar of the White Admiral feeding on Fly Honeysuckle.

1

2

3

Southern White Admiral

1

Limenitis reducta

(Aristocrats)

Description: Wingspan 4.4-5.2 cm. Upperside shimmering blue-black with white bands which are formed from a series of spots; underside similar to that of the Poplar Admiral (see p. 26) but colours more intense and pattern more sharply defined.

Distribution: Southern Europe, up to 1600 m, only in very mild localities north of the Alps; on the dry edges of woods and in shrubby areas.

Flight period: Mid-May to Aug or Sep; one or two broods.

Behaviour: Warmth-loving species, often seen sunning itself on leaves with wings outspread; eggs laid singly on the caterpillar's food plant along the midrib of the leaf.

Caterpillar: Green with longitudinal white stripes, underside and claspers dark red, back with two rows of red-brown spines. Feeds on Fly Honeysuckle and other honeysuckles. Forms a grey suspended chrysalis.

Hibernation: As a young caterpillar, enclosed in a rolled-up, cylindrical section of leaf.

Purple Emperor 🦋

2

Apatura iris

(Aristocrats)

Description: Wingspan 6-7.4 cm. Dark brown with white bands and spots, only the ♂ (right picture) iridescent purple; undersides (small picture) orange-brown with white bands and spots and an eye-spot on forewing.

Distribution: Europe except for northern Scandinavia, the north of Great Britain, and large parts of southern Europe; in open riverine and mixed woodlands up to 1500 m, most often alongside streams, rivers or lakesides.

Flight period: Mid-June to late Aug; one brood.

Behaviour: Flies usually at treetop level, only coming down to the ground for water and food; feeds on wet patches of soil, carrion, excrement and tree sap; eggs laid singly on the upperside of leaves of the caterpillar's food plant.

Caterpillar: Brown at first, when fully grown green with oblique yellow streaks, with two red-tipped horns at the head end, otherwise smooth and shaped like a slug. Feeds mainly on sallow, but also on other species of willow and various poplars; rests in the middle of the leaf surface, relying on its camouflage. Chrysalis green, suspended from the underside of a leaf.

Hibernation: As a young caterpillar, on a silk pad nestling against a twig of the food plant.

The Purple Emperor's wings have a brightly coloured underside.

1

2

Comma ⚥

Polygonia c-album

(Aristocrats)

Description: Wingspan 4.5-5 cm. Wing outline strikingly jagged; upperside with dark brown to black spots on a reddish-brown ground-colour; underside (small picture) indistinctly dappled brown, with a small white 'c' on hind wing.

Distribution: Throughout Europe, except northwest Scandinavia, up to 1900 m; edges of woods and clearings, water meadows and shrubby countryside, not uncommon even in gardens.

Flight period: Mid-June to Oct, and after hibernation Mar to mid-May; two broods.

Behaviour: Visits flowers, but also feeds on tree sap and fruits; ♀ lays eggs singly on leaves.

Caterpillar: Black with orange-red banding and a large white spot on the back (resembling a bird dropping), with strong spines. Feeds singly on hops and nettles, and sometimes on elm, Gooseberry and Red Currant. Forms a slender, grey-brown, suspended chrysalis.

Hibernation: As an adult butterfly.

Note: The jagged outline of the wing and the bark-like pattern of the underside provide excellent camouflage for the butterfly when at rest.

Camberwell Beauty (⚥)

Nymphalis antiopa

(Aristocrats)

Description: Wingspan 6-6.5 cm. Dark velvety-brown, with a broad yellow margin (fading to whitish after hibernation), preceded by a row of blue spots; underside dark grey-brown with a whitish margin.

Distribution: Europe except for northwest Scandinavia, a rare immigrant to the British Isles, up to 2000 m; in riverine woods and open mixed forests, and on shrubby shaded slopes.

Flight period: Mid-July to late Sep, and after hibernation from Mar to June; one brood.

Behaviour: Visits flowers and also feeds on tree sap, ripe fruits, and damp soil; ♂ patrols, often along forest rides, whilst searching for ♀; eggs laid in dense rows around twigs; often inactive during the hottest weeks of summer (aestivation).

Caterpillar: Black with black spines and a row of rusty-red spots on the back. Lives gregariously in a loosely woven silk 'nest' on sallow and other willow species as well as various birch species; forms a brownish-grey suspended chrysalis.

Hibernation: As an adult butterfly.

The Comma derives its name from the small white 'c' on the underside of the hind wing.

1

2

1 Large Tortoiseshell (⚥)   *Nymphalis polychloros*
(Aristocrats)

Description: Wingspan 5.4-6.4 cm. Orange-red with black spots and lighter yellowish areas, with a black margin that has blue spots only on hind wing; underside dappled brown, resembling bark (small picture).

Distribution: Throughout Europe except for the far north, very rare in Britain, up to 1500 m or more; at the edges of woods and in open countryside with isolated trees or bushes, parks.

Flight period: Mid-June to late July and again, after hibernation, from Mar to late May; one brood.

Behaviour: Flight rapid and impetuous; feeds on flowers, in spring on sallow catkins and tree sap; eggs laid around the tips of twigs.

Caterpillar: Black, with yellow to orange longitudinal stripes, with strong spines. Lives gregariously in a loose silken web, mainly on elm and sallow but also on willows as well as various other trees. Suspended chrysalis golden-brown with shining metallic spots, formed away from the host tree and located among ground vegetation, on fences, dry branches or stones.

Hibernation: As an adult butterfly.

2 Small Tortoiseshell ⚥   *Aglais urticae*
(Aristocrats)

Description: Wingspan 4-5 cm. Orange-red, pattern of spots more extensive than in the Large Tortoiseshell, with a small white spot at tip of forewing, margins of both wings always with distinct blue spots; underside brown, forewing with large sand-coloured areas.

Distribution: Throughout Europe, from the sea coast up to 3000 m; in gardens, parks, hedgerows, fallow land, and wherever the caterpillar's food plant grows. Very common.

Flight period: Mid-May to late Sep and again, after hibernation, from Feb or Mar to May; two or three broods, but only one at higher altitudes.

Behaviour: Visits flowers; eggs laid in batches on the underside of young leaves. Butterflies of the second and third generations commonly migrate, covering distances of more than 100 km from where they hatch.

Caterpillar: Black with yellow longitudinal stripes, with spiny hairs. Feeds only on stinging nettles; caterpillars live in a communal silken web up to the last moult, and thereafter live singly; suspended chrysalis grey-brown with

shining golden spots, often formed at some distance from the food plant and attached to a plant stem.

Hibernation: As an adult butterfly, in sheltered corners, not uncommonly in cellars, barns, attics (associated with cultivated areas).

The underside of the Large Tortoiseshell wing resembles bark and renders the resting butterfly very inconspicuous.

Painted Lady 🦋

Cynthia (Vanessa) cardui

(Aristocrats)

Description: Wingspan 5-6 cm. Pale orange with black spots, also with white spots on forewing; underside of hind wing with a row of five eye-spots (small picture).

Distribution: Throughout Europe, up to 2000 m; almost everywhere during the migratory season, but thereafter mainly in open countryside, including gardens.

Flight period: Immigrants from Apr; then two or three broods from June to Oct; return migration in autumn.

Behaviour: Feeds on flowers and fallen fruit; eggs laid singly on leaves of the caterpillar's food plant.

Caterpillar: Grey or black, with yellow stripes on the sides. Feeds on various thistles, nettles, mallows, and many other plants; it draws leaves together with silk and feeds inside this protective tent. Hanging chrysalis within the web, grey-brown with shining golden spots.

Hibernation: As an adult butterfly, but only south of the Alps.

Note: Regularly migrates in spring and usually in small groups from southern Europe northwards across the Alps. Populations increase greatly over the summer and then die out in autumn.

Map Butterfly

Araschnia levana

(Aristocrats)

Description: Wingspan 3.2-4 cm. Spring brood red-brown on upperside with black spots (picture 2); summer brood black-brown with white bands; undersides of wings russet with a network of pale lines that gives this butterfly its name (picture 3).

Distribution: Over a broad belt from France through central Europe to temperate eastern Europe, not over 1000 m, rare and in isolated pockets in southern Europe; in water meadows and open, moist, mixed forests, preferring shaded areas.

Flight period: Late Apr to mid-June, and early July to late Aug; two broods.

Behaviour: A very active butterfly; feeds on flowers; ♀ lays batches of green cylindrical eggs in little 'towers' on the underside of nettle leaves.

Caterpillar: Black, with strong spines. Lives gregariously beneath leaves of nettles. Hanging chrysalis grey-brown.

Hibernation: As a chrysalis.

Note: Whether the chrysalis continues to develop or enters hibernation depends on day length whilst the caterpillar is feeding, and the colour of the resulting butterfly is thus determined mainly by the ambient temperature.

When viewed from below, the bright red forewings of the Painted Lady are usually mainly concealed.

1

2

3

1   Red Admiral 🦋   *Vanessa atalanta*

(Aristocrats)

Description: Wingspan 5-6 cm. Black-brown with red bands and white spots; underside of forewing similar to upperside, underside of hind wing dappled grey-brown (small picture).

Distribution: Throughout Europe except the far north, up to 2000 m; usually in wooded countryside such as open woods, parks, gardens.

Flight period: Migrants from the south arrive in northern Europe in May, otherwise two or three broods from July to Oct.

Behaviour: Feeds eagerly on fallen fruit and tree sap, and also on flowers; usually opens and closes its wings vigorously whilst feeding; ♀ lays eggs singly on leaves of the caterpillar's food plant.

Caterpillar: Varies in colour from black through greenish grey to yellow-brown, with more or less distinct spots and with short spines. On stinging nettle, where it feeds singly inside a protective tent of leaves held together with silk. Chrysalis grey-brown with shining golden spots, suspended from the underside of a leaf.

Hibernation: As an adult butterfly, but only in isolated cases north of the Alps. Some butterflies try to migrate back south in the autumn.

Note: When assisted by the wind, butterflies can migrate up to several thousand kilometres northwards. Usually a solitary flyer when migrating.

2   Peacock 🦋   *Inachis io*

(Aristocrats)

Description: Wingspan 5.5-6 cm. Ground-colour red, each wing with a large multi-coloured eye-spot; underside of wings blackish brown.

Distribution: Throughout Europe except for northern Scandinavia, up to 2000 m; in gardens, orchards and parks, along the flower-rich edges of woods, in damp meadows and scrub.

Flight period: Late June to Oct, and after hibernation Mar to June; one or two broods.

Behaviour: Feeds on nectar at many kinds of flower; ♀ lays eggs in small batches on the underside of leaves of the caterpillar's food plant.

Caterpillar: Black with numerous white dots and shining black spines. Feeds gregariously on nettles and hops, and at other times stays within a protective web; chrysalis green or grey-brown, hanging in cracks and crevices in bark or walls.

Hibernation: As an adult butterfly in sheltered spaces such as tree holes or attics.

When at rest the Red Admiral covers its colourful forewings with the inconspicuous hind wings.

1 Two-tailed Pasha *Charaxes jasius*

(Aristocrats)

Description: Wingspan of ♂ 6.5-7.5 cm, of ♀ 8-9 cm. Hind wing with two narrow points. Upperside dark brown with an orange outer margin, underside (picture) with a bright vivid pattern.

Distribution: In Mediterranean countries; mainly in coastal regions, in dry hilly countryside up to 800 m.

Flight period: May to Sep; two broods.

Behaviour: Flight very rapid and usually high above the ground; feeds on rotting fruit, carrion or excrement; commonly rests on the outer branches of the Strawberry tree; defends its territory against not only other individuals of the same species but also against other butterflies; ♀ lays eggs singly on the upperside of leaves of the caterpillar's food plant.

Caterpillar: Bright green with small yellow dots and lines along sides, with two eye-spots on the back, and four reddish-brown spines on head; hind end forked. Feeds only on the Strawberry tree, where the blue-green hanging chrysalis can be found.

Hibernation: As a caterpillar on evergreen plants.

2 Silver-washed Fritillary ⌸ *Argynnis paphia*

(Fritillaries)

Description: Wingspan 5.6-6.5 cm. ♂ (picture) bright orange with black spots and streaks, ♀ with a darker pattern, underside mainly olive-green in ground-colour, hind wing with silvery bands.

Distribution: Throughout most of Europe, absent only from Crete, southern Spain and northern Scandinavia, in mountains to over 1500 m; mainly on the edges of woods, in clearings and in water meadows.

Flight period: Late June to mid-Sep; one brood.

Behaviour: Feeds at flowers, especially thistles and other composites; ♂ carries out a complicated mating display during which the antennae of the ♀ come into contact with the scent-scales on his forewings: this special scent induces the ♀ to mate; eggs are laid singly on tree trunks close to the caterpillar's food plants.

Caterpillar: Black-brown with two orange-yellow lines on back, with long reddish-brown spines. Feeds on Dog Violet, Hairy Violet and other violet species; usually feeds at night and conceals itself by day, often at some distance from the food plant; hanging chrysalis usually among the ground vegetation.

Hibernation: As a tiny caterpillar, usually in the crevices of tree bark.

The caterpillar of the Silver-washed Fritillary feeds only on violets.

1 Dark Green Fritillary 🦋 *Argynnis aglaja*
(Fritillaries)

Description: Wingspan 5-6 cm, ♀ distinctly larger than ♂. Upperside very similar to that of the Silver-washed Fritillary (see p. 38), but underside of hind wing overlaid with a greenish colour and a large number of roundish silver spots that shimmer like mother-of-pearl.

Distribution: Throughout Europe, in mountains up to the tree line, sometimes above 2000 m; along the edges of woods and in clearings, on moors and in unimproved meadows.

Flight period: Mid-June to late Aug; one brood.

Behaviour: Visits flowers, especially thistles and other composites; eggs laid singly on leaves or stems of the caterpillar's food plant.

Caterpillar: Blackish with silver-grey longitudinal stripes when young; velvet-black with a row of orange-red spots along each side and black spines when mature. Feeds on various species of violet and Wild Pansy; feeds at night and remains concealed by day, often at some distance from the food plant. Chrysalis suspended among the ground vegetation, attached to a few leaves or grass stalks drawn together with silk.

Hibernation: As a young caterpillar at the base of the food plant.

Similar Species: The High Brown Fritillary 🦋 (*Argynnis adippe*) is similar but has small reddish-ringed spots on underside of hind wing.

2 Queen of Spain Fritillary (🦋) *Argynnis lathonia*
(Fritillaries)

Description: Wingspan 3.6-4.8 cm. Similar to the Dark Green Fritillary, but distinctly smaller and outer margin of forewing slightly concave; undersides (small picture) with unusually shiny silver spots, even at tip of forewing.

Distribution: A migratory butterfly which flies northwards from southern Europe every year, occasionally reaching England and central Scandinavia in favourable years; up to 2500 m in the Alps; prefers rough areas, heaths, stubble fields, dry sandy localities, and coastal dunes.

Flight period: Mid-Apr to early Nov; two or three broods, but only one at higher altitudes.

Behaviour: A very rapid flyer; visits flowers, especially thistles and other composites; ♀ lays eggs singly on the leaf-stalk of the caterpillar's food plants.

Caterpillar: Black with a double white line on the back, with reddish-brown spines. Feeds on violet and Wild Pansy. Chrysalis golden-brown with light stripes, suspended among the ground vegetation.

Hibernation: North of the Alps as a caterpillar, further south also as a chrysalis or adult butterfly.

The light spots on the underside of the Queen of Spain Fritillary really shimmer like mother-of-pearl.

1

2

Lesser Marbled Fritillary

Brenthis ino

(Fritillaries)

Description: Wingspan 3.6-4.2 cm. A pattern of black spots and stripes on an orange-red ground-colour; underside of forewing resembling upperside but paler, hind wing with a pattern of patches and loops, with a narrow stripe overlaid with blue-violet on middle of wing.

Distribution: Scattered localities in northern, central and southeast Europe, in mountains up to 2000 m, absent from the British Isles; in damp, open woodlands, swampy meadows and peat bogs.

Flight period: Late May to mid-Aug; one brood.

Behaviour: The ♂ makes regular patrolling flights whilst searching for ♀; ♀ lays the yellowish, red-brown striped eggs singly on the underside of leaves of the caterpillar's food plants.

Caterpillar: Yellowish grey-brown with a broad whitish stripe on sides and six rows of yellowish spines. Feeds mainly on Meadowsweet, but also on Great and Salad Burnet and several other plants; generally feeds at night, but also by day when the weather is overcast; occasionally suns itself on the ground vegetation. Chrysalis yellowish brown with shining metallic spots; suspended.

Hibernation: As an egg in which the young caterpillar is ready to hatch.

Note: Sometimes ♀ occur that are particularly dark dusted blue-black.

Marbled Fritillary

Brenthis daphne

(Fritillaries)

Description: Wingspan 4.3-4.8 cm. Upperside very similar to that of the Lesser Marbled Fritillary, underside (picture 3) extensively overlaid with blue to violet on hind wings.

Distribution: Southern and southeast Europe up to 1400 m, but very local in western and central Europe; in open mixed forests and along the shrubby edges of woods.

Flight period: Late May to mid-Aug; one brood.

Behaviour: Visits flowers; ♂ defends his territory against competitors; ♀ lays eggs singly on the leaves of the caterpillar's food plants.

Caterpillar: Black-brown with a double yellowish line on the back and yellow side stripes, orange spines with black hairs at tips. Feeds on blackberry and raspberry bushes. Suspended chrysalis yellow-grey with shining metallic notches on the back, usually placed close to the ground.

Hibernation: Usually as an egg within which the young caterpillar is ready to hatch; sometimes as a young caterpillar on or close to the food plant.

Note: A subspecies that lives in the southern valleys of the Alps (picture 2) is distinctly larger and has a finer black pattern on a lighter ground-colour.

1 Shepherd's Fritillary

Boloria pales

(Fritillaries)

Description: Wingspan 3.2-3.8 cm. Ground-colour of ♂ (picture) a vivid orange-red, ground-colour of ♀ more or less overlaid with greenish grey, the black pattern rather fine.

Distribution: Isolated localities in the Alps, Pyrenees, Carpathians and Caucasus, between 1500 m and 3000 m; in flower-rich alpine meadows and pastures above the tree line, sometimes very common.

Flight period: Mid-June to mid-Sep; one brood.

Behaviour: A striking hovering flight close to the ground; visits flowers; eggs laid singly on the caterpillar's food plant.

Caterpillar: Black-brown with a double yellowish line on the back and rows of deep black, yellow-edged spots, yellowish spines with black bristles. Feeds mainly on species of violet. Chrysalis brownish grey, suspended, on and beneath stones.

Hibernation: As a young caterpillar in a fine web, and usually for a second winter as a half-grown caterpillar.

Similar species: The Mountain Fritillary (*Boloria napaea*, picture 2) also has the same distribution and abundance; it is rather larger with an even finer black pattern; ♀ (picture) generally overlaid with dark greenish to blackish. Flies only until mid-Aug.

3 Bog Fritillary

Proclossiana eunomia

(Fritillaries)

Description: Wingspan 3.4-4 cm. Yellow-brown to orange with a pattern of black dots and streaks, underside of wings (small picture) without mother-of-pearl spots.

Distribution: Northern and northeast Europe, patchily in central Europe, from lowlands up to 1500 m; in damp, swampy meadows, generally on the margins of peat bogs.

Flight period: Late May to mid-July, in some years also in Sep; one brood.

Behaviour: Feeds at flowers, especially Common Bistort; eggs laid in small batches on the underside of leaves of the caterpillar's food plant.

Caterpillar: Grey-brown with reddish spines. Gregarious when young, but solitary later; feeds at night on Common Bistort; conceals itself by day beneath leaves or in the ground litter. Chrysalis grey-brown with shining silver spots, suspended.

Hibernation: Usually through two winters, once as a half-grown and then as a fully grown caterpillar.

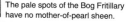

The pale spots of the Bog Fritillary have no mother-of-pearl sheen.

1

2

3

Small Pearl-bordered Fritillary 🦋

(Fritillaries) *Clossiana (Boloria) selene*

Description: Wingspan 3.5-4.2 cm. With a pattern of black streaks and dots on a bright orange-red background, underside of hind wings (small picture) and tips of forewings with a colourful assembly of yellow, white and brown patches.

Distribution: Throughout Europe except for Ireland and the extreme south, in mountains to over 2000 m; along the edges of woods, on shrubby slopes, water meadows, and damp meadows, sometimes very common.

Flight period: Mid-May to mid-Sep; two broods, but only one at higher altitudes and in the north.

Behaviour: Feeds at flowers on nectar, most eagerly on scabious and Wild Thyme; ♀ lays eggs singly on the underside of violet leaves.

Caterpillar: Reddish- or blackish-brown with a black head, small white dots, ochre-brown spines and black hairs; shade loving, and feeds singly on various species of violet, especially Dog Violet and Marsh Violet. Chrysalis yellow-brown with shining metallic spots, suspended, among the ground vegetation.

Hibernation: As a caterpillar in a rolled-up leaf.

Pearl-bordered Fritillary 🦋

(Fritillaries) *Clossiana (Boloria) euphrosyne*

Description: Wingspan 3.5-4.5 cm. Similar to the Small Pearl-bordered Fritillary, but underside of hind wing with predominantly ochre-yellow and brown-red areas and a central silver spot (picture 3).

Distribution: Widespread throughout Europe except for southern Spain, up to 2000 m; at the edges of woods and forest rides, also dry meadows and heaths.

Flight period: Late Apr to early Aug; one brood, locally in the south with two broods.

Behaviour: Similar to that of the Small Pearl-bordered Fritillary.

Caterpillar: Black-brown, with a yellow, sometimes bluish, interrupted side-stripe and short black spines and hairs. Feeds on Marsh Violet, Dog Violet and other species of violet. Suspended chrysalis, attached to other plants in the ground layer.

Hibernation: As a caterpillar inside a curled-up leaf of the food plant.

The undersides of the Small Pearl-bordered Fritillary's wings look like a small mosaic.

1   Glanville Fritillary ⚘   *Melitaea cinxia*

(Fritillaries)

Description: Wingspan 3.4-4.2 cm. ♀ (picture) larger and usually darker than ♂. Uppersides of wings yellowish brown with a black, lattice-like pattern; underside (small picture) of forewing mainly ochre-yellow, of hind wing with dotted bands of ochre-yellow and whitish.

Distribution: Europe except for southern Spain, the British Isles (only in Isle of Wight) and the far north, from lowlands to over 1700 m; in unimproved meadows, rough dry areas and roadside embankments.

Flight period: Mid-May to July, with one brood; or until Aug, with two broods.

Behaviour: Visits flowers; eggs laid on the underside of leaves of the caterpillar's food plants.

Caterpillar: Black with small white dots, head and false legs red-brown, spines short and black. Lives gregariously in a silken web, feeding on plantains and other plants. Chrysalis suspended, light grey with yellowish warts, attached to plant stems.

Hibernation: As a half-grown caterpillar in a communal silk web.

2   # False Heath Fritillary   *Melitaea diamina*

(Fritillaries)

Description: Wingspan 3.4-4.2 cm. Upperside of ♂ (picture) red-brown with a thick black-brown lattice-like pattern; ♀ on the whole rather lighter, the pattern containing yellowish features; underside of hind wings with brightly coloured patches and a row of dark dots.

Distribution: Europe, except for southern Italy, Iberian Peninsula, British Isles, northern Scandinavia, in mountains up to 2000 m; in damp meadows, bogs and high moors.

Flight period: Late May to late Aug; one brood.

Behaviour: Visits flowers; ♀ lays yellowish eggs in small batches on leaves of the caterpillar's food plants.

Caterpillar: Almost black with short, orange-yellow spines. Remains concealed in the ground vegetation by day, but comes out in the afternoon and climbs up its food plants, valerian, cow-wheat and plantain. Chrysalis china-white with a pattern of black and orange stripes and dots, suspended, among the ground vegetation, under stones or in rocky crevices.

Hibernation: As a young caterpillar, in a communal silk web beneath dry leaves.

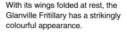

With its wings folded at rest, the Glanville Fritillary has a strikingly colourful appearance.

1 **Knapweed Fritillary** *Melitaea phoebe*
(Fritillaries)

Description: Wingspan 4-4.8 cm. Upperside similar to that of many other Fritillaries; underside almost as in the Glanville Fritillary (see p. 48) but without black dots in the bands.

Distribution: Southern and southern central Europe, up to 2000 m in the Alps; in dry countryside.

Flight period: Mid-May to early Sep; one brood.

Behaviour: Visits flowers; eggs laid in several batches on the leaves of the caterpillar's food plant.

Caterpillar: Black-grey with whitish dots and whitish-yellow or red-brown side-stripes, with abundant spines. Feeds on the Greater Knapweed and other knapweed species; lives gregariously in a silken web when young, but solitary later. Chrysalis brown, suspended.

Hibernation: As a caterpillar, in groups under dry leaves.

2 **Spotted Fritillary** *Melitaea didyma*
(Fritillaries)

Description: Wingspan 3.5-4.5 cm. ♂ fiery-red with small black spots and a black-white fringe, ♀ (picture) dull red to brownish, with a more or less dense black or grey pattern; undersides of wings (small picture) with orange to yellowish bands (whitish in ♀) and black spots.

Distribution: Europe except for Scandinavia, British Isles, Netherlands and northern Germany, up to 2000 m in mountains; in meadows, dry forest clearings, mountain slopes, always in sunny and warm localities.

Flight period: Mid-May to late Sep; one to three broods.

Behaviour: Visits flowers to feed; eggs laid in two layers, one on top of the other, on the underside of leaves of the caterpillar's food plants.

Caterpillar: Rather brightly coloured, with whitish dots and lines on blue-grey background, spines orange-red and with black hairs. Feeds singly on plantains, toadflax, speedwells, and many other species of herbaceous plants. Chrysalis whitish, with black and orange streaks, commonly suspended from the food plant.

Hibernation: As a caterpillar, on the food plant.

Note: Varies greatly in colour and pattern, which has given rise to numerous geographical subspecies.

When at rest, the Spotted Fritillary displays the distinctively patterned underside of its wings.

50

1 ## Little Fritillary

Mellicta asteria

(Fritillaries)

Description: Wingspan 2.6-2.8 cm. Black pattern on upperside of wings rather extensive, giving a dark impression; the orange-brown ground-colour rather paler in ♀; underside similar to that of the Meadow Fritillary (picture 2).

Distribution: Restricted to the High Alps, between 2000 and 3000 m; in alpine meadows.

Flight period: Early July to late Aug; one brood.

Behaviour: With a peculiar hovering flight; visits flowers; eggs laid in several layers on the underside of leaves of the caterpillar's food plant.

Caterpillar: Black, with a delicate yellow pattern and yellowish false legs, spiny. Feeds on Alpine Plantain. Chrysalis rather stout, brightly chequered, suspended from the food plant.

Hibernation: As a caterpillar, generally over two winters.

Similar species: The rather larger Meadow Fritillary (*Mellicta parthenoides*, picture 2 and small picture) is found in southwest and western Europe and southern central Europe, from lowlands to about 1800 m. Its caterpillar is black, with red-brown spines; it feeds and overwinters on plantain species.

3 ## Heath Fritillary 🦋

Mellicta athalia

(Fritillaries)

Description: Wingspan 3.5-4 cm. Upperside of wings with a black-brown lattice-like pattern on an ochre-yellow to intensely orange background, undersides with orange, white and yellow patches.

Distribution: Throughout Europe, except southern Spain, in mountains to over 2000 m; on the edges of woods, forest rides and clearings, also in damp meadows.

Flight period: Mid-May to Aug, with one brood; south of the Alps until Sep, with two broods.

Behaviour: Feeds at flowers on nectar, especially on thistles and umbels, often flitting in some numbers around the blooms; usually spends the night on flowers or grass stems; courtship and mating generally in late afternoon; ♀ lays eggs in small batches on the underside of leaves.

Caterpillar: Black with small white dots and thick, ochre-yellow spines. Lives and feeds on Field Cow-wheat and other herbaceous plants; gregarious when young, solitary later. Chrysalis whitish with black and brown spots, suspended, among the ground vegetation.

Hibernation: As a young caterpillar, in a communal web among the dead leaves of herbaceous plants.

Note: A very scarce and local butterfly in southern England.

Like its closest relatives, the Meadow Fritillary commonly visits flowers.

1

2

3

Marsh Fritillary 🦋

(Fritillaries)   *Eurodryas (Euphydryas) aurinia*

Description: Wingspan 3.2-4.3 cm. With a contrasting pattern of red-brown and ochre-yellow, black-edged areas; undersides with a similar pattern but paler.

Distribution: Almost throughout Europe (absent from northern Scandinavia and some Mediterranean areas), from lowlands up to 1500 m; mainly in damp meadows and moors.

Flight period: Early May to mid-July; one brood.

Behaviour: Feeds at flowers; ♀ lays lemon-yellow eggs which later turn brown, in densely packed batches on the underside of leaves of the caterpillar's food plants.

Caterpillar: Black, with whitish dotted stripes on the back and sides, with black spines. Feeds mainly on Devil's-bit Scabious, but also on plantains; gregarious when young, living in silken webs which often cover the entire plant; solitary when fully grown, commonly sunning itself on the ground or on grasses. Chrysalis white with black spots, suspended, among the ground vegetation.

Hibernation: As young caterpillars, in a protective communal silk web, usually on low plants close to the food plant.

Note: Extremely variable in size, colour and pattern, and forming a whole series of geographical subspecies.

Cynthia's Fritillary

(Fritillaries)   *Hypodryas (Euphydryas) cynthia*

Description: Wingspan 3.6-4.4 cm. ♂ (picture 2) with a pattern of white spots on upperside that varies greatly between individuals, ♀ without white spots; underside of wings (picture 3) with whitish and orange-brown bands.

Distribution: In the Alps between 1500 m and 3000 m; in flower-rich meadows.

Flight period: Late June to end Aug; one brood.

Behaviour: Visits flowers; ♀ lays eggs in batches on the leaves of the caterpillar's food plants.

Caterpillar: Black, with a fine yellow pattern, body and the thick spines with black hairs. Lives gregariously on Alpine Plantain, Lady's-mantle and Long-spurred Pansy. Chrysalis silver-grey with a black pattern, suspended.

Hibernation: Passes a first winter as a young caterpillar, in a communal protective web, and a second winter as a fully grown caterpillar, singly beneath stones or grass tufts.

The caterpillar of the Marsh Fritillary lives mainly on Devil's-bit Scabious.

1

2

3

Marbled White 🦋   *Melanargia galathea*

(Browns)

Description: Wingspan 4-5 cm. Upperside with a chessboard pattern of black and white; underside with less-contrasting markings, ♂ grey-white and ♀ yellowish white.

Distribution: Southern, southeast and central Europe (absent from Iberian Peninsula), from lowlands to over 1800 m; in unimproved and unfertilised meadows, and the edges of woods.

Flight period: Late May to early Sep; one brood.

Behaviour: Feeds at flowers, especially composites such as thistles or knapweeds; ♂ begins flying early in the morning, skimming low over grasses whilst searching for a ♀; eggs laid on the soil.

Caterpillar: Pale brown or yellowish green with brown head, dark lines on back and sides, with short hairs. Feeds mainly on Upright Brome, but also on many other species of grass; remains concealed by day; changes its food plants according to their nutritional content. Chrysalis yellowish grey, on the ground and generally in the middle of a grass tuft.

Hibernation: As a newly hatched caterpillar or after the first moult.

Alpine Grayling   *Oeneis glacialis*

(Browns)

Description: Wingspan 4.6-5.5 cm. Beige, russet to blackish (individuals vary) with a dark margin, forewing with one or two dark eye-spots and hind wing with one, underside (picture 3) of hind wing with striking pale veins on a dark ground-colour.

Distribution: In the Alps between 1500 m and 3000 m; on steep rocky slopes.

Flight period: Late May to late August; one brood.

Behaviour: Feeds at flowers on nectar, especially on tufts of pinks; often rests on the ground; ♂ vigorously defends its territory against other ♂, usually from an isolated rock or stone; eggs laid singly on dry grass stems.

Caterpillar: Reddish brown with black stripes on back and sides, with two short points at hind end. Feeds mainly on Sheep's Fescue, and probably on other species of grass at high altitudes. Chrysalis roundish, lying freely on the soil.

Hibernation: As a caterpillar, generally through two winters.

Note: Only appears abundantly every other year.

The caterpillar of the Marbled White feeds on grasses, on Tor Grass in this picture.

1

2

3

The Dryad

Minois dryas

(Browns)

1

Description: Wingspan 4.8-6.2 cm. ♂ (picture) dark brown, each forewing with two black eye-spots with pale blue centres, sometimes hind wing also with a small spot; ♀ rather larger and ground-colour lighter than in ♂.

Distribution: Central, eastern and southeast Europe, up to 1500 m; in meadows, open woods, and scrub-covered hills.

Flight period: Early July to mid-Sep; one brood.

Behaviour: Flies in early morning and again in late afternoon; with a slow and heavy fluttering flight, usually just above the ground; feeds at flowers on nectar; ♀ drops her eggs to the ground whilst in flight.

Caterpillar: Yellowish grey, with dark stripes on back and sides, with a forked tail, without hairs, head brown. Feeds on Upright Brome, Meadow Fescue, Wood Small-reed, Purple Moor-grass and other grasses. Chrysalis flattened and brown, resting on the ground at the base of the host grass.

Hibernation: As a caterpillar, on the food plant.

Note: One of the few butterflies that occurs equally in wet and dry habitats.

The Hermit

Chazara briseis

(Browns)

2

Description: Wingspan 4.6-5.8 cm. Dark grey-brown, with a dirty white interrupted band across fore- and hind wing, the forewing band enclosing two dark eye-spots (larger in ♀, which sometimes has three); undersides (picture) spotted with shades of grey and brown.

Distribution: Southern and southern central Europe up to 1500 m; on sunny, rocky slopes of short grass, scree slopes, quarries, steppe-like meadows and in karst areas, generally on limestone.

Flight period: June to mid-Sep; one brood.

Behaviour: A skilful and rapid flyer; feeds at flowers on nectar; often rests in direct sunlight on the ground or on stones (wings closed when at rest and providing excellent camouflage on stones); ♀ lays eggs singly on grass stems.

Caterpillar: Dark brown to yellowish grey, with blackish longitudinal stripes, tapering towards hind end and ending with two short tails, without hairs. Feeds on Upright Brome, Sheep's Fescue, Blue Moor-grass and other tough grasses, crawling from tuft to tuft but in general not very active. Chrysalis stout, brown, shining, enveloped in a kind of cocoon, in the soil at the base of a grass tuft.

Hibernation: As a caterpillar.

Note: A series of geographic forms can be recognised, which differ from each other by the variable development of their pale wing spots or by their orange spots.

1 Great Banded Grayling

Brintesia circe

(Browns)

Description: Wingspan 6-7.4 cm. Dark brown, with a sharply defined white band that breaks up into spots on forewing; the first of these spots containing a dark eye-spot; ♂ (small picture) rather smaller than ♀ and with a narrower band; undersides (picture, right) with dappled ground-colour, resembling bark.

Distribution: Central and southern Europe, but rare and localised north of the Alps, up to 1500 m; in dry meadows and clearings in deciduous woods, sunny edges of woods, and wooded or shrubby slopes.

Flight period: Late June to early Sep; one brood.

Behaviour: Feeds at flowers or ripe fruit; rests on tree trunks, with wings closed and forewings pulled back between hind wings (underside of hind wings providing excellent camouflage); ♀ drops eggs singly among grasses.

Caterpillar: Brown, with brown stripes and a thin black line on the back, head light yellow with black stripes, a short forked tail at hind end, without hairs. Feeds on grasses such as Upright Brome and Sheep's Fescue. Chrysalis in a silken cocoon in the soil or at the base of a grass tuft.

Hibernation: As a young caterpillar.

2 Grayling 🏳

Hipparchia semele

(Browns)

Description: Wingspan 4.8-6 cm. Brown with a yellowish band, forewing with two dark eye-spots, hind wing with one; hind wing with underside dappled like bark or stone (picture).

Distribution: Throughout Europe except for northern Scandinavia, up to 2000 m; in warm, dry, sandy locations such as open pine forests, heaths, dunes.

Flight period: Late June to mid-Oct; one brood.

Behaviour: Flight low and powerful; rests with wings closed on stones or tree trunks; feeds on tree sap, and also on nectar; ♂ with a rapid courtship flight, followed by a complex courtship ritual; ♀ lays eggs singly on young grass stems.

Caterpillar: Pale brown with darker stripes, a short forked tail, without hairs. Feeds at night on Upright Brome, Sheep's Fescue, and other grasses, remaining concealed on the ground by day. Chrysalis in a cocoon just under the soil surface.

Hibernation: As a caterpillar.

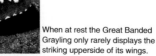

When at rest the Great Banded Grayling only rarely displays the striking upperside of its wings.

Arran Brown

Erebia ligea

(Browns)

Description: Wingspan 4-4.8 cm. Dark brown, with an orange band containing small eye-spots, fringes alternating light and dark; ground-colour of ♀ lighter brown than ♂ (picture 1); underside of hind wing with a narrow, irregular white band that resembles a splash of cream (picture 2).

Distribution: Northern, central and southeast Europe, in the Alps and other mountain ranges but not above 1700 m; in damp deciduous woods, forest rides and clearings, and in flower-rich stream gullies.

Flight period: Late June to late Aug; one brood.

Behaviour: Feeds at flowers on nectar; on overcast days rests amongst grasses with wings closed, but opens them out when the sun shines, warming up more rapidly by exposing the dark uppersides; eggs laid singly on dry grass stems.

Caterpillar: Pale grey-brown with a dark stripe on the back and pale stripes on sides, short points at hind end, with short hairs. Feeds on Wood Sedge, Moor-grass species and other grasses. Chrysalis brown with a black pattern, lying freely on the soil.

Hibernation: As an egg (occasionally as a newly hatched caterpillar), and then through a second winter as a fully grown caterpillar.

Scotch Argus 🦋

Erebia aethiops

(Browns)

Description: Wingspan 3.8-4.8 cm. Upperside very similar to that of the Arran Brown but fringes uniformly light brown, underside of hind wings with a broad grey band which is often very weakly marked in ♂ (picture).

Distribution: Central and eastern Europe including the British Isles, absent from the Mediterranean area and Scandinavia; in open woodland, forest meadows, and the flower-rich edges of woods, up to 2000 m.

Flight period: Early June to late Sep; one brood.

Behaviour: Similar to that of the Arran Brown.

Caterpillar: Light brownish grey, with a black interrupted line along sides, with short hairs. Feeds on Upright Brome, Tor Grass, Purple Moor-grass, Sheep's Fescue, Wood Small-reed and other grasses. Chrysalis on the ground.

Hibernation: As a young caterpillar in the ground vegetation.

The caterpillar of the Scotch Argus feeds on various grasses, including Sheep's Fescue as shown here.

1 Yellow-spotted Ringlet
Erebia manto

(Browns)

Description: Wingspan 3.6–4.2 cm. Wings dark brown, ♂ (picture) with an orange-red band which in ♀ is more ochre-yellow and partly broken up into spots; underside mid-brown with irregular orange- or ochre-yellow spots.

Distribution: In the Alps, Vosges, Pyrenees and Carpathians, between 1200 m and 2500 m; in flower-rich alpine meadows, generally close to the tree line.

Flight period: Late June to mid-Aug; one brood.

Behaviour: Feeds at flowers on nectar; eggs laid singly on grass stems.

Caterpillar: Greenish ochre-brown with rows of black comma-shaped streaks, with black bristles. Feeds on Sheep's Fescue and other grass species; active at night, resting concealed on the ground by day. Chrysalis ochre-yellow with a black pattern, lying freely on the ground.

Hibernation: As a caterpillar.

2 Woodland Ringlet
Erebia medusa

(Browns)

Description: Wingspan 4–4.8 cm. Dark brown to almost black, each wing with a row of black eye-spots surrounded by orange-yellow and with white centres; underside resembling upperside; ♀ with paler ground-colour and eye-spots rather larger than in ♂ (picture).

Distribution: Central and northern Europe up to 2600 m; in damp unfertilised meadows with tall vegetation close to the edges of woods or copses, also in boggy meadows.

Flight period: Early May to early Aug; one brood.

Behaviour: Feeds at flowers on nectar; ♀ lays eggs singly on grass stems.

Caterpillar: Grass-green with a black line on back, small pointed tips at hind end, with short bristles. Feeds on Upright Brome, Red and Sheep's Fescue, and other grass species; feeds only at night, remaining concealed on the ground by day. Chrysalis stout, beige with dark brown stripes and dots; upright on the ground in the middle of a grass tuft.

Hibernation: As a half-grown caterpillar in the ground vegetation.

Note: Several geographical subspecies are known, including butterflies without any pattern of spots and eyes.

Similar species: The Almond-eyed Ringlet (*Erebia alberganus*, picture 3) flies in the Alps, usually in grass-rich meadows between 1000 m and 1300 m; the orange wing spots are more oval, and the black eye-spots are smaller. The dark green caterpillar feeds on Sheep's Fescue, Sweet Vernal Grass and other grasses.

1

2

3

Mountain Ringlet    *Erebia epiphron*
(Browns)

Description: Wingspan 3-3.5 cm. Ground-colour dark brown with an orange band across the wings containing a row of small eye-spots; band and eye-spots larger in ♀ (picture) than in ♂.

Distribution: In the mountains of Europe (except Scandinavia), usually between 1200 m and 2500 m; in flower-rich alpine meadows and open stands of dwarf shrubs.

Flight period: Late June to mid-Aug; one brood.

Behaviour: Flight slow, just above the ground; rests on grass stems or flowers, feeding on nectar (especially at Arnica and hawkweed); ♀ lays eggs singly on stems of the larval host grasses.

Caterpillar: Light green with a dark line on back and yellowish stripes on sides, head dark green, small points at hind end, with short bristles. Feeds almost entirely at night, mainly on Alpine Hair-grass but also on other grasses. Chrysalis light green with whitish hind end; on the ground.

Hibernation: As a caterpillar.

Note: In Britain confined to mountain grassland in Scotland and the English Lake District.

Large Ringlet   *Erebia euryale*
(Browns)

Description: Wingspan 3.8-4.4 cm. Ground-colour dark brown, wing bands highly variable, from ochre-yellow through russet-brown to orange-red, on hind wing usually broken up into individual spots; ♀ (picture) with colours generally lighter and more contrasting than in ♂, especially on underside (small picture).

Distribution: In the coniferous forest zone of the European mountains, between 800 m and 2400 m; on the flower-rich edges of woods, in clearings and alpine meadows.

Flight period: Mid-June to late Aug; one brood.

Behaviour: Similar to that of the Mountain Ringlet.

Caterpillar: Pale ochre-brown with a blackish line on the back. Feeds on Wood Meadow-grass, Glaucous Sedge and other grasses. Chrysalis yellowish with a dark pattern, on the ground.

Hibernation: As a caterpillar, often through two winters.

Note: A series of geographical subspecies have been recognised which differ mainly in the extent and colour of the wing bands.

The wing bands of the Large Ringlet are highly variable in extent and colour.

1 Silky Ringlet

Erebia gorge

(Browns)

Description: Wingspan 3.4-3.8 cm. Upperside black-brown, forewing with a broad russet band that encloses black eye-spots with white centres; forewing with underside (picture) mainly russet-brown, hind wing mottled brown.

Distribution: European mountains (except Scandinavia), on rocky and stony slopes between 1600 m and 3000 m; mainly in localities poor in vegetation such as scree slopes.

Flight period: Early July to late Aug; one brood.

Behaviour: Flies only on sunny days, frequently resting on warm rocks and stones; feeds on nectar from flowers growing in rocky crevices, especially on hawkweeds; ♀ lays eggs singly on grass stems.

Caterpillar: Mainly green with a black, white-bordered stripe on the back. Feeds at night on Small Meadow-grass and species of moor-grass and fescue. Chrysalis flattened, pale brown with light green wing-sheaths, on the ground.

Hibernation: As a caterpillar, through two winters.

Note: As with other dark brown mountain butterflies, the dark colour of the wings is a way of absorbing the sun's warmth. As soon as the sun begins to shine, the butterfly opens its wings, which are otherwise folded together when at rest, and begins to 'warm up'.

2 Swiss Brassy Ringlet

Erebia tyndarus

(Browns)

Description: Wingspan 3.2-3.8 cm. Brown, forewing with a russet spot enclosing one or two small black eye-spots; underside of forewing with an extensive russet-red area, hind wing marbled grey-brown; shimmering metallic (mainly green) in the sunlight; ♀ on the whole more yellowish, the shining effect weaker than in ♂ (picture).

Distribution: In the Alps and Carpathians, between 1600 m and 3000 m; in sheltered spots on short-turfed alpine meadows and on sunny grassy slopes.

Flight period: Early July to late Sep; one brood.

Behaviour: Similar to that of the Silky Ringlet.

Caterpillar: Grey-green to dark grey-brown with a dark stripe on back, with dark lines and dots on sides, with short tails at hind end, with short hairs. Feeds singly on Mat Grass and on fescue species; feeds at night, remaining concealed on the ground by day. Chrysalis plump, brown, on the ground.

Hibernation: As a caterpillar.

Note: The reflecting scales are not distributed evenly over the wing surface. So according to the direction of the light and the viewing angle, the butterfly may shimmer with the most diverse colours or may appear wholly dull brown.

Ringlet 🦋

(Browns)

Aphantopus hyperantus

Description: Wingspan 3.8-4.8 cm. Upperside black-brown, usually with two small eye-spots on each wing and whitish fringes; undersides (small picture) lighter brown with black, yellow-ringed eye-spots.

Distribution: Europe except for Scandinavia and some parts of the Mediterranean area, not above 1600 m; on the edges of woods and in clearings, on north-facing slopes and in damp, lush meadows; very common at suitable sites.

Flight period: Early June to late Aug; one brood.

Behaviour: Visits flowers, often in huge numbers, especially umbels, Blackberries and Raspberries; hardly ever exposes the wing uppersides; ♀ drops eggs to the ground whilst in flight.

Caterpillar: Grey-brown with a blackish line on the back, with short hairs. Feeds singly on Upright Brome, Red Fescue, Tor Grass, Cocksfoot and other grasses; active at night. Chrysalis stout, brown-striped, placed upright between loose silken threads at the base of a grass tuft.

Hibernation: As a half-grown caterpillar in the ground vegetation.

Meadow Brown 🦋

(Browns)

Maniola jurtina

Description: Wingspan 4-5 cm. Ground-colour dark brown, forewing with one eye-spot each on upper- and underside, ♀ (picture) with a long patch on upperside of forewing that varies from ochre-yellow through orange to red-brown; underside of forewing russet-red, of hind wing marbled grey-brown.

Distribution: Throughout Europe except the far north, up to 1800 m; in meadows and pastures, along field banks, grassy slopes and woodland edges; common everywhere.

Flight period: Mid-May to Oct; one brood; inactive for several weeks in the Mediterranean area during the hottest and driest period of the summer (aestivation).

Behaviour: Flies during sunny and overcast weather; visits flowers both to feed on nectar and to rest; before laying eggs, the ♀ inspects several potential breeding sites; eggs laid singly on grass stems and on dry material close to the ground.

Caterpillar: Grass-green, grey-green below, with fine hairs. Feeds on Upright Brome, Red Fescue, Smooth Meadow-grass, and other grass species. Chrysalis yellowish green with a dark pattern, suspended from grass stems.

Hibernation: As a caterpillar.

The undersides of the Ringlet wings have striking yellow-edged eye-spots.

1

2

1 # Gatekeeper 🦋   *Pyronia tithonus*

(Browns)

Description: Wingspan 3.2-4 cm. Uppersides of wings orange-red inside with a broad brown edge, forewing with a black eye-spot with two white centres; underside of forewing (picture right) like the upperside, hind wing with a beige-brown pattern. The ♂ (small picture) rather smaller than ♀, with more intense colours.

Distribution: Central and southern Europe, including British Isles, not above 1100 m; in open deciduous woods, hedgerows, heaths and pine forests, at the edge of high moors; local, but sometimes common.

Flight period: Early July to late Sep; one brood.

Behaviour: Feeds at flowers; commonly found around bramble thickets, where the ♂ displays striking territorial behaviour (perches on a shrub or tall plant and investigates the other butterflies that come within its range); eggs laid singly on grass leaves.

Caterpillar: Creamy white with a fine ochre-brown pattern and dark brown line on back, head light brown, forked tail small, with short hairs. Feeds on Perennial Ryegrass, Timothy Grass, bents, fescues and other grasses; active at night, concealed on the ground by day. Chrysalis angular, pale greenish grey, with a black pattern, attached to grass stems.

Hibernation: As a young caterpillar in the ground vegetation.

2 # Large Heath 🦋   *Coenonympha tullia*

(Browns)

Description: Wingspan 3-4.4 cm; ♀ slightly larger and paler than ♂. Ground-colour of upperside varying from pale orange-brown to dark brown with paler markings; forewing with one or two eye-spots, hind wing with up to four eye-spots, sometimes none; underside (picture) usually with black, white-ringed eye-spots, but in some forms these are very pale and inconspicuous.

Distribution: Northern and central Europe, up to 2000 m; in bogs, mosses, wet moorland, and damp hillsides.

Flight period: Mid-June to late Aug; one brood.

Behaviour: Flies slowly, but active in both dull and sunny weather; visits flowers; eggs laid at the base of grass tussocks.

Caterpillar: Green with yellowish white lines along back and sides. Feeds

on Harestail Grass, White-beaked Sedge and related plants. Chrysalis green with conspicuous black stripes, suspended from a stem.

Hibernation: As a caterpillar, sometimes through two winters.

Note: Many subspecies of this highly variable butterfly have been described.

The eye-spots at the tip of the wing of the Gatekeeper enclose two white dots.

1 Pearly Heath

Coenonympha arcania

(Browns)

Description: Wingspan 3.2-3.8 cm. Ground-colour dark brown, forewing orange except for a broad brown margin; underside (picture) with an irregular white band and several eye-spots of unequal size on hind wing.

Distribution: Europe, except for Spain, northern Scandinavia and the British Isles, from lowlands up to 1200 m; mainly in hilly country, at dry shrubby woodland edges, meadows and slopes.

Flight period: Mid-May to late Aug, with one brood; locally south of the Alps until Sep with two broods.

Behaviour: Flies mostly at head-height around bushes; rests on the leaves of bushes and small trees, always with wings closed; ♀ lays relatively large yellow eggs singly on the stems of the caterpillar's food plants.

Caterpillar: Green with yellowish longitudinal stripes and reddish tips at hind end, more or less without hairs. Feeds on Yorkshire Fog, Tor Grass, Sheep's Fescue, and species of meadow-grass and melick. Chrysalis stout, pale green or grey-green with a pattern of dark lines and dots, suspended from a grass stem just above ground level.

Hibernation: As a caterpillar.

2 Small Heath 🦋

Coenonympha pamphilus

(Browns)

Description: Wingspan 3.2-3.6 cm. Wings yellowish orange to deep orange with grey fringes, eye-spot at tip of forewing small and black on upperside, larger and highlighted by being enclosed in a yellow circle on underside (picture), underside of hind wing with an inconspicuous grey-brown pattern.

Distribution: Throughout Europe except for the far north, from lowlands to over 1800 m; everywhere in meadows that are neither very damp nor very dry.

Flight period: Mid-Mar to mid-Oct; two or three broods, but only one brood at higher altitudes.

Behaviour: With a slow fluttering flight, usually just above the ground vegetation; frequently rests on the ground or on grass stems, more rarely on flowers; eggs laid singly at the base of grasses.

Caterpillar: Green with thin longitudinal lines and a pale forked tail, with stubbly hairs. Feeds mainly at night on several bent-grasses, fescues, Smooth Meadow-grass and other grasses. Chrysalis stout, green, suspended from a pad of silk on a grass stem.

Hibernation: As a young caterpillar on the ground.

Note: One of the most abundant butterflies in central Europe.

1

2

Speckled Wood 🦋 *Pararge aegeria*

(Browns)

Description: Wingspan 4-4.5 cm. Wings brown with pale yellow spots, especially on forewings; forewing with one eye-spot, hind wing with three; in ♀ (picture 2) the pattern of yellowish spots more extensive than in ♂ (picture 1); underside of hind wing marbled brown-yellow. The intensity of the colour varies greatly from place to place.

Distribution: Throughout Europe except for the far north, up to 1200 m in the mountains; in open deciduous woods, on the edges of woods, in clearings and along forest rides.

Flight period: Mid-Mar to Oct; two or three broods.

Behaviour: Prefers to remain in shade and half-shade; readily rests on the leaves of shrubs and herbaceous plants; feeds on nectar and the juice of overripe berries, also on excrement and flowing tree sap; ♂ vigorously defends his territory against intruders; ♀ lays eggs singly on grass stems and leaves of the caterpillar's food plants.

Caterpillar: Matt green with a short, pale forked tail, with very short hairs. Feeds on Wood Sedge, False Brome, Bearded Couch, Cocksfoot, Yorkshire Fog, and other species of grass. Chrysalis green or dark brown, suspended from the base of grass stems or beneath loose stones.

Hibernation: As a chrysalis, but occasionally as a caterpillar.

Woodland Brown *Lopinga achine*

(Browns)

Description: Wingspan 4.5-5.5 cm. Grey-brown, along the wing margins with a row of black eye-spots enclosed in yellow rings; undersides (small picture) lighter, fringed with a yellowish double line, eye-spots as on upperside but more contrasting and with white centres.

Distribution: In temperate Europe, absent from southern and northern Europe and from Great Britain, not occurring above 1500 m; mainly in open deciduous and mixed woods with a rich ground vegetation.

Flight period: Late May to late Aug; one brood.

Behaviour: Keeps generally to the edges of woods, avoiding deep shade and open sunshine; rests on the leaves of trees and shrubs; ♀ drops her eggs onto the ground.

Caterpillar: Grass green with whitish tips at hind end, with short hairs.

Feeds on False Brome, Soft-leaved and White-flowered Sedge, and other grasses. Chrysalis green, attached to a grass stem by silk.

Hibernation: As a half-grown caterpillar, on the ground.

The underside of the Woodland Brown is embellished with contrasting streaks and curls.

1

2

3

1 Wall Brown 🦋 *Lasiommata megera*

(Browns)

Description: Wingspan 3.8-4.5 cm. Brown with orange areas which are more extensive and intense in colour in ♀ (picture) than in ♂ and with small eye-spots, underside (small picture) with a striking eye-spot at tip of forewing and with fine ochre and grey-brown marbling on hind wing.

Distribution: Throughout Europe except for northern Scandinavia, up to 1500 m; in warm, dry, open habitats such as road and hedge banks, ruins, rocky slopes and heaths.

Flight period: Mid-Apr to late Oct; two or three broods.

Behaviour: Flies rapidly close to the ground, preferring sunny habitats; often rests on stones or walls warmed by the sun; spends the night on the ground beneath overhanging grasses; ♀ lays eggs singly on the caterpillar's food plants.

Caterpillar: Green with numerous tiny white dots, small points at hind end, with short hairs. Feeds on Tor Grass, Cocksfoot, Sheep's Fescue, Upright Brome and other grasses. Chrysalis grass-green, suspended from a grass stem or a stone.

Hibernation: As a half-grown caterpillar.

2 Large Wall Brown *Lasiommata maera*

(Browns)

Description: Wingspan 4.5-5.2 cm. Brown, with a band of russet-red spots along outer margins of wing which contain one large eye-spot at tip of forewing and two or three smaller ones on hind wing, these all black with white centres; russet-red pattern more strongly developed in ♀ (picture) than in ♂; undersides similar to those of the Wall Brown.

Distribution: Throughout Europe except for northern Scandinavia and the British Isles, up to 2000 m; in warm, dry, rocky habitats, but also along the edges of woods, in unimproved meadows and pastures.

Flight period: Early May to late Sep; one or two broods.

Behaviour: Similar to that of the Wall Brown.

Caterpillar: Grass-green, with short hairs. Feeds on Common Bent, Red Fescue, Sheep's Fescue and other grass species. Chrysalis whitish green or black, suspended from rocks or grass stems.

Hibernation: As a caterpillar.

Similar species: The very similar but somewhat smaller Northern Wall Brown (*Lasiommata petropolitana*, picture 3) flies in the Alps between 800 m and 2000 m, from early May to late July.

The Wall Brown has many eye-spots on the wing undersides.

1

2

3

Duke of Burgundy Fritillary 🦋

(Blues)   *Hamearis lucina*

Description: Wingspan 2.5-3.4 cm. With rows of orange, more or less angular spots on a dark brown background; underside (small picture) lighter, with two striking rows of pearly white spots on hind wing.

Distribution: Central and southern Europe except for southern Spain and southern Italy, especially in lowlands but also in mountains up to 1400 m; in woodland meadows, the edges of woods and scrubby countryside.

Flight period: Early Apr to mid-July; one brood, but two south of the Alps.

Behaviour: Flight not particularly rapid; commonly conceals itself on the underside of large leaves; feeds on nectar, but is not a common flower visitor (these butterflies are fairly short lived); ♀ lays spherical shining eggs singly or in small batches on the underside of Primrose leaves.

Caterpillar: Slug-like in shape, yellowish brown with rows of small black-brown spots, with fine hairs. Feeds at night on Cowslip, Oxlip and primrose, remaining concealed by day on the underside of leaves or in the leaf litter below the food plant. Chrysalis whitish, with black spots and long fine hairs; attached by a silken girdle to the food plant.

Hibernation: As a chrysalis.

Green Hairstreak 🦋

                                              Callophrys rubi

(Hairstreaks)

Description: Wingspan 2.5-3 cm. Upperside brown and inconspicuous, underside entirely green.

Distribution: Throughout Europe, up to 2000 m in mountains; in open woods, in dry shrubby areas and on heaths.

Flight period: Early Apr to late Aug; one or two broods.

Behaviour: Flight very rapid but only in short bursts; rests amongst leaves, where the folded wings provide good camouflage; feeds on flowers and also on honeydew; ♂ territorial; ♀ lays eggs singly on the flowers or young shoots of the caterpillar's food plants.

Caterpillar: Woodlouse-shaped, intensely green with a pattern of whitish-yellow lines, with short hairs. Feeds on a variety of plants, such as broom, Gorse, Dogwood, Crowberry and Common Rockrose. Chrysalis brown, roundish, on the ground beneath the food plant. It can produce a creaking or scratching sound. This sound is believed to be attractive to ants which feed on its secretions.

Hibernation: As a chrysalis.

Duke of Burgundy Fritillaries mating.

1 ## Brown Hairstreak 🏵   *Thecla betulae*
(Hairstreaks)

Description: Wingspan 3.5-4 cm. Hind wing with small tails; upperside dark brown with small orange spots near the tails, ♀ (small picture) with a large orange patch on forewing; underside (picture right) cinnamon-brown with fine whitish transverse streaks.

Distribution: Europe, except for Mediterranean region and northern Scandinavia, not above 1500 m; in open deciduous woods, on shrubby slopes, also in orchards; not uncommon.

Flight period: Early July to mid-Oct; one brood.

Behaviour: Flies mainly around the tops of trees and shrubs, resting in the sun on leaves; feeds on nectar and honeydew; ♀ lays round, chalk-white eggs singly on forks or cracks in the bark of twigs of the caterpillar's food plants.

Caterpillar: Stout, intensely green with a pattern of yellow lines, with short hairs. Feeds mainly on Sloe, but also on Plum, Wild Cherry and other deciduous trees. Chrysalis smooth, brownish, lying freely on the ground.

Hibernation: As an egg.

2 ## Black Hairstreak 🏵   *Strymonidia pruni*
(Hairstreaks)

Description: Wingspan 3-3.2 cm. Upperside dark brown, some orange spots along the edge of hind wing and, in ♀, on forewing too; underside of wings (picture) mid-brown, edges orange-red with a pattern of black dots.

Distribution: Central Europe, with isolated localities in southern England and southern Scandinavia, not above 1200 m; on warm and sunny slopes with stands of Sloe, occasionally also in orchards.

Flight period: Late May to late July; one brood.

Behaviour: Feeds at flowers on nectar, especially at Blackberry, Raspberry, Elder and Privet; ♀ lays dirty-white eggs singly on the bark of the caterpillar's food plant, generally where the twigs fork.

Caterpillar: Short and stout, light green with small brownish warts on the back. Feeds mainly on Sloe, but also on fruit trees such as different kinds of plum; consumes buds, flowers and young leaves. Chrysalis with a bizarre jagged outline, black-brown with a white 'saddle', attached by a silken girdle to the upperside of leaves and twigs (where it resembles a bird dropping).

Hibernation: As an egg.

Only the ♀ of the Brown Hairstreak has an orange patch on the forewing.

1

2

White-letter Hairstreak ♫ *Strymonidia w-album*

(Hairstreaks)

Description: Wingspan 2.6-3.2 cm. Upperside black-brown; underside (picture) dark brown, hind wing with thin white lines in the shape of a 'W', outer edge with orange-red U-shaped spots and tails.

Distribution: Europe except for the Iberian Peninsula and northern Scandinavia, from lowlands up to 1200 m; in open countryside with trees, parks, water meadows, and the edges of woods with elms.

Flight period: Early June to early Sep; one brood.

Behaviour: Flies mainly around the tops of elm trees; feeds on nectar, mainly at umbels; eggs discus-shaped, transparent at middle, and laid singly on elm twigs, usually at the base of buds.

Caterpillar: Woodlouse-shaped, light green when first hatched, becoming darker later, with short hairs. Feeds on English Elm, Wych Elm and other species of elm, consuming buds, flowers and young leaves. Chrysalis compact, brownish, attached to the bark by a girdle.

Hibernation: As an egg.

Ilex Hairstreak *Nordmannia ilicis*

(Hairstreaks)

Description: Wingspan 2.8-3.4 cm. Upperside brown, forewing with an orange patch which is distinctly smaller in ♂ than in ♀, and is often absent; underside (picture) somewhat lighter in ground-colour, with a thin, broken, white line parallel to the wing-margin and small orange spots at the edge of hind wing.

Distribution: Central and southern Europe, absent from large areas of the Iberian Peninsula, from lowlands up to 1400 m; warm, dry areas at the edges of woods, clearings, and shrubby hillsides with young oaks.

Flight period: Early June to mid-Aug; one brood.

Behaviour: Feeds on nectar at flowers; eggs laid singly on the bark of slender oak twigs.

Caterpillar: Woodlouse-shaped, light green, with short hairs. Feeds on Pedunculate Oak and other species of oak. Chrysalis brownish with dark dots, attached by a girdle to the ground vegetation.

Hibernation: As an egg, occasionally as a young caterpillar.

Further species: The Purple Hairstreak ♫ (*Quercusia quercus*) has the

upperside of its wings shot with iridescent purple, more prominently so in ♂ (small picture). Widespread in Europe. The caterpillar feeds on oak.

The Purple Hairstreak has the upperside of its wings shot with iridescent purple.

1

2

Small Copper 🔲   *Lycaena phlaeas*
(Coppers)

Description: Wingspan 2.5-3 cm. Forewing yellow- to red-orange with a broad, dark brown margin and black spots, hind wing black-brown with a jagged orange marginal band; underside of forewing orange-brown with a grey margin and black spots, hind wing grey-brown with dark spots. Individuals of the summer brood are generally darker than others.

Distribution: Throughout Europe to northernmost Scandinavia, and up to 2000 m in mountains; in dry sunny unimproved meadows, cattle pastures, fallow land, and other flower-rich areas where sorrel and dock grow.

Flight period: Early Apr to early Nov; two to four broods.

Behaviour: A nimble flyer, usually solitary; feeds on nectar at a wide variety of flowers; generally rests with wings half-open; ♂ defends his territory vigorously against other butterfly intruders; ♀ lays eggs singly on the base of sorrel and dock leaves.

Caterpillar: Woodlouse-shaped, green, sometimes with broad rosy stripes, with short hairs. Feeds on various species of sorrel and dock, remaining concealed on the underside of leaves. Chrysalis ochre-brown with black dots, attached to the underside of leaves of the food plant.

Hibernation: As a young caterpillar, occasionally still as an egg.

Scarce Copper   *Lycaena (Heodes) virgaureae*
(Coppers)

Description: Wingspan 3-3.5 cm. Upperside of ♂ (picture right) shining orange-red with a black border, with a golden sheen; ♀ (small picture) yellowish orange with black spots, without a golden sheen; undersides ochre-yellow to grey with small black and white spots.

Distribution: Central Europe, also in isolated localities in the Iberian Peninsula, up to 2400 m in the Alps; in damp, flower-rich meadows, the edges of woods and clearings.

Flight period: Mid-June to mid-Sep; one brood.

Behaviour: Similar to that of the Small Copper.

Caterpillar: Woodlouse-shaped, dark green with yellowish stripes. Feeds on Common and Sheep's Sorrel. Chrysalis smooth, brownish and dark speckled, attached to the food plant.

Hibernation: As an egg, with the caterpillar ready to hatch.

Similar species: The Large Copper (🔲) (*Lycaena dispar*) has pale bluish-grey undersides to hind wing. Found in central and southern Europe (became extinct in England, but has been reintroduced).

The ♀ of the Scarce Copper lacks the golden sheen of the ♂.

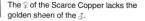

1

2

Sooty Copper

Lycaena (Heodes) tityrus

(Coppers)

Description: Wingspan 2.5-3.2 cm. Upperside of ♂ black-brown with black spots and a fine white fringe, forewing of ♀ (picture 1) orange in ground-colour, margin of hind wing with an orange band.

Distribution: Central and southern Europe, up to 2500 m in mountains; in dry meadows and forest clearings, steppe-like countryside, often on sandy soils.

Flight period: Mid-Apr to early Sep; two broods, but only one at higher altitudes.

Behaviour: Visits flowers; ♀ lays green eggs singly on the underside of sorrel and dock leaves.

Caterpillar: Short, light green, sometimes even purple-violet, with fine white dots and reddish hairs. Feeds on various species of sorrel and dock. Chrysalis smooth, greenish or brown, finely dark-speckled, attached to the food plant.

Hibernation: As a caterpillar.

Note: At over 1000 m in the Alps there is a distinct subspecies which is particularly dark in both sexes; the ♀ lacks all trace of orange (picture 2).

Purple-edged Copper

Lycaena hippothoe

(Coppers)

Description: Wingspan 3-3.6 cm. Upperside of ♂ (picture right) red-gold with black margins and white fringes, overlaid with a violet sheen; ♀ similar to the ♀ of the Sooty Copper, but less contrasting; underside (small picture) light grey-brown, sometimes marked with orange, with many white-ringed black spots.

Distribution: Western and northern Europe, in the south only in mountains to over 2000 m, absent from the British Isles; in wet meadows, lowland moors and damp alpine pastures.

Flight period: Early June to early Sep; generally one brood.

Behaviour: Feeds on nectar at flowers; eggs laid singly at the base of sorrel and dock leaves.

Caterpillar: Woodlouse-shaped, green, with short hairs. Feeds mainly on Common Sorrel, but also on Sheep's Sorrel; active at night, remaining concealed beneath leaves by day. Chrysalis yellow-brown with black dots, lying freely on the ground.

Hibernation: As a caterpillar.

Note: A subspecies that flies at high altitude in the Alps lacks the violet sheen and can be easily confused with the Scarce Copper (see p. 86).

The Purple-edged Copper has a striking pattern of dots on the underside.

1

2

3

Chalk-hill Blue 🦋

Lysandra coridon

(Blues)

Description: Wingspan 3-3.5 cm. Upperside of ♂ (picture 1) pale silver-blue with brown margins and white fringes, ♀ (picture 2) brown with white fringes; underside similar to that of the Adonis Blue but with a lighter ground-colour.

Distribution: Throughout Europe except Scandinavia and the south of Spain and Italy, up to some 2000 m in mountains; in warm dry habitats such as unimproved meadows, railway embankments or field banks, generally on chalk soils.

Flight period: Mid-June to Oct; one brood.

Behaviour: A rapid flyer; often in large numbers where it occurs, territorial; feeds at flowers on nectar; spends the night resting on flowers or with head down on grass stems; ♀ lays eggs singly on dry grass stems close to the caterpillar's food plant, or at the base of the food plant itself.

Caterpillar: Short and stout, grey-green with two rows of yellow spots and a shining black head, with short hairs. Feeds mainly on Horseshoe Vetch, also on Crown Vetch, Milk Vetch and Wild Liquorice, remaining concealed by day beneath stones or in moss at the base of the food plant. Secretions from its 'honey gland' attract ants which protect it from enemies in exchange for this 'honey'. Chrysalis rather slender, smooth, olive-brown, on the ground or beneath stones.

Hibernation: As an egg, with the caterpillar ready to hatch.

Adonis Blue 🦋

Lysandra bellargus

(Blues)

Description: Wingspan 2.8-3.4 cm. Upperside of ♂ (picture right) a vivid sky-blue; ♀ very similar to ♀ of the Chalk-hill Blue, sometimes even overlaid with blue; undersides (small picture) light brown, with orange spots and black white-ringed dots.

Distribution: Europe except for Scandinavia, in mountains up to 2000 m; like the Chalk-hill Blue, in dry and sandy habitats with sparse vegetation.

Flight period: Mid-Apr to early Oct; two broods.

Behaviour: Like that of the Chalk-hill Blue.

Caterpillar: Resembling that of the Chalk-hill Blue but darker green. Feeds only on Horseshoe Vetch.

Hibernation: As a young caterpillar on the food plant.

In both sexes of the Adonis Blue, the underside of the wings is brown in ground-colour with a vivid pattern.

1

2

3

Common Blue 🦋 *Polyommatus icarus*

(Blues)

Description: Wingspan 2.7-3.4 cm. Upperside of ♂ (picture right) light blue, with a violet tinge and a white fringe; ♀ (small picture) brown, occasionally overlaid with blue, with a row of orange spots along outer wing-margins; underside light grey in ♂, light brown in ♀, with a vivid pattern of dots in both sexes.

Distribution: Throughout Europe to the Arctic, in mountains to over 2000 m; in dry and wet meadows, in open hilly country.

Flight period: Early Apr to mid-Oct; two or three broods.

Behaviour: Feeds on flowers, but also at damp patches on the ground; at night, rests head-down on grass stems; ♀ lays eggs singly on the buds or flowers of the caterpillar's food plants.

Caterpillar: Woodlouse-shaped, pale green with thin, yellowish side stripes and short hairs. Feeds especially on Bird's-foot Trefoil, but also on Lucerne, medicks, restharrows and other plants; frequently visited by ants which feed on secretions produced by glands at the hind end and protect it from enemies. Chrysalis smooth, shining olive-brown, on the ground below the food plant.

Hibernation: As a half-grown caterpillar.

Mazarine Blue (🦋) *Cyaniris semiargus*

(Blues)

Description: Wingspan 2.6-3.4 cm. Upperside of ♂ (picture) violet-blue with brown margins and brown-dusted veins, ♀ dark brown; undersides light grey-brown with small, black, white-ringed dots.

Distribution: Throughout Europe except for the British Isles (where it became extinct and now only occurs as a rare vagrant), to over 2500 m in mountains; in damp, flower-rich meadows in thinned-out forests.

Flight period: Mid-May to mid-Oct; two or three broods, but only one at higher altitudes.

Behaviour: Feeds at flowers on nectar; ♀ lays greenish-blue eggs in short rows among flowers of the caterpillar's food plants.

Caterpillar: Woodlouse-shaped, green with darker longitudinal stripes, with short hairs. Feeds principally on Red Clover, also on Zigzag Clover and Kidney Vetch, consuming flower buds and blooms and later the young leaves. Chrysalis olive-brown, on the stem of the food plant.

Hibernation: As a young caterpillar.

The brown ♀ of the Common Blue has rows of delicate orange dots.

Green-underside Blue

Glaucopsyche alexis

(Blues)

Description: Wingspan 2.8-3.4 cm. Upperside of ♂ (picture 1) violet-blue with blackish-brown outer edges, of ♀ (picture 2) black-brown, generally overlaid with blue in the area close to the body, usually with a white fringe; underside of each forewing (small picture) with a row of large, black, white-ringed dots, hind wing overlaid with blue or turquoise at base.

Distribution: Central and southern Europe, but very local in northern Germany, Denmark and the Netherlands, up to 2000 m in the Alps; in dry shrubby meadows and woodland clearings, at the sunny edges of woods.

Flight period: Mid-Apr to early July, with one brood; in the south, flies until Aug with two broods.

Behaviour: Feeds at flowers on nectar; ♀ lays eggs singly on flowers and buds of the caterpillar's food plants.

Caterpillar: Greenish or cream, with a dark line on back and oblique stripes on sides, with relatively long and dense hairs. Feeds mainly on Lucerne and sainfoin, but also on Crown Vetch, Tufted Vetch, Dyer's Greenweed and other plants. Ants are attracted to and feed on the secretions from glands at the hind end; they also protect the caterpillar from enemies. Chrysalis green-brown, inconspicuous, on the food plant.

Hibernation: As a fully grown caterpillar, sometimes as a chrysalis.

Small Blue 🦋

Cupido minimus

(Blues)

Description: Wingspan 2-2.6 cm. Upperside of ♂ (picture) dark brown, dusted blue at wing-base (extent and shade of blue very variable), ♀ wholly dark brown, wings sometimes white-fringed; underside grey with small black dots.

Distribution: Throughout Europe except for northern Europe and southern Spain, up to 3000 m in mountains; in unimproved meadows and dry, unfertilised areas.

Flight period: Early Apr to early Sep; two or three broods, but only one brood at higher altitudes.

Behaviour: Often present in large numbers where it occurs; feeds at flowers on nectar; eggs laid within flowers of the caterpillar's food plant.

Caterpillar: Pale brown to grey-green, with short hairs. Feeds on Kidney

Vetch and related plants, consuming flowers and seeds. Chrysalis greenish yellow with black dots, usually on a grass stem.

Hibernation: As a caterpillar in a withered flower.

The underside of the wing-base in the Green-underside Blue alternates between blue and turquoise.

1

2

3

1 # Silver-studded Blue 🦋   *Plebejus argus*
(Blues)

Description: Wingspan 2.5-3 cm. Upperside of ♂ (picture) blue, enclosed by a more or less broad black band and with a white fringe, upperside of ♀ dark brown with a broken orange band; both sexes with underside light brown, hind wing with a band of bright orange and a marginal row of black spots with shining metallic centres.

Distribution: Throughout Europe except for the far north, in mountains to over 2000 m; in sunny unimproved meadows, sandy heaths, dry shrubby limestone grassland and high moors.

Flight period: Mid-June to Sep; one or two broods.

Behaviour: Flies within well-defined areas but often in large numbers; feeds at flowers on nectar and at wet patches on the ground; large numbers may aggregate to spend the night, with heads down on stalks and grass stems; ♀ lays eggs singly on the caterpillar's food plant.

Caterpillar: Relatively slender, grey-green to red-brown, with a dark white-edged stripe on back, with short hairs. Feeds on flowers and leaves of Bird's-foot Trefoil, Crown Vetch, Rockrose, Heather and other plants; active at night, spending the day concealed on the ground; always attended by ants which feed on secretions from glands at the hind end and protect it from enemies. Chrysalis pale green with a dark line on back, at base of food plant.

Hibernation: As an egg.

2 # Brown Argus 🦋   *Aricia agestis*
(Blues)

Description: Wingspan 2.2-2.8 cm; ♀ slightly larger and more brightly marked than ♂. Upperside dark brown with white fringes, band of orange spots present on margin of forewing and hind wing (picture).

Distribution: Central and southern Europe, in mountains up to 900 m; heaths, dunes and downland.

Flight period: Apr to Aug; two or three broods.

Behaviour: Flies rapidly in sunny weather; eggs laid singly on the uppersides of leaves of the caterpillar's food plants.

Caterpillar: Short and stout, green with a whitish line along sides. Feeds on Rockrose, stork's-bills and crane's-bills; attended by ants.

Hibernation: As a caterpillar.

Similar species: The Northern Brown Argus 🦋 (*Aricia artaxerxes*) can be distinguished by the presence of a white spot in the centre of the forewing and less brightly coloured markings. Has a more northerly distribution than the Brown Argus.

The Geranium Argus (*Eumedonia eumedon*) has a similar underside to the Silver-studded Blue.

1 Large Blue (⚥)

Maculinea arion

(Blues)

Description: Wingspan 3.2-4 cm. Upperside blue with black-brown margins and black spots, in ♀ margins broader and spots larger than in ♂ (picture); underside ochre-brown with many black spots.

Distribution: Central and southern Europe to southern Scandinavia (became extinct in British Isles but has been reintroduced), up to 2000 m in mountains; on close-cropped pastures, bare clearings and dry meadows.

Flight period: Early June to mid-Aug; one brood.

Behaviour: Generally flies singly; feeds at flowers on nectar; ♀ lays eggs on flower buds of the caterpillar's food plants.

Caterpillar: Short and stout, rosy when young, becoming pale ochre-brown with a black head, with sparse hairs. Feeds at first on Wild Thyme or Marjoram, eating the flowers and ripening seeds, then lives in underground ants' nests, where the yellowish-brown chrysalis is to be found later.

Hibernation: As a caterpillar, in ants' nests.

Note: The caterpillars of this and the other two Blues on this page leave their food plants in late summer and are carried off by certain ant species into their nests. There they feed on the grubs and pupae of the ants. In return they provide their 'hosts' with a sweet nutritious secretion from the glands at their hind end.

2 Alcon Blue

Maculinea alcon

(Blues)

Description: Wingspan 3.3-3.6 cm. Upperside of ♂ (picture) blue with black-brown wing-margins; ♀ grey-brown with some dark spots on forewing; undersides similar to the Large Blue.

Distribution: As for the Large Blue, but only up to 1500 m; in damp meadows, moors, sandhills.

Flight period: Early July to late Aug; one brood.

Behaviour: As for the Large Blue.

Caterpillar: Light green or reddish brown with dark head. Lives at first in the calyx or seed vessels of Marsh Gentian and Willow Gentian, and later in the underground nests of various ant species, where the chrysalis is also found.

Hibernation: As a caterpillar, in ants' nests (see note for Large Blue).

3 Scarce Large Blue

Maculinea teleius

(Blues)

Description: Wingspan 2.8-3.6 cm. Uppersides blue with some black spots and broad black edges, which are even broader in ♀ than in ♂ (picture); underside ochre-brown with many black spots.

Distribution: In the east of central Europe, up to 2000 m; in rather dry habitats, the sides of paths and ditches where Great Burnet grows, but also in peaty meadows.

Flight period: Mid-June to mid-Aug; one brood.

Behaviour: As for the Large Blue.

Caterpillar: Purple-brown with tiny black warts. First lives on Great Burnet flowers, later in ants' nests where the chrysalis is also to be found.

Hibernation: As a caterpillar, in ants' nests (see note for Large Blue).

1

2

3

1 Holly Blue ⌘ *Celastrina argiolus*

(Blues)

Description: Wingspan 2.8-3.4 cm. Upperside sky-blue, ♀ (picture) with broad black-brown wing-margins; underside bluish silver-grey with small black dots.

Distribution: Throughout Europe except for the far north, in mountains up to 1600 m; in forest clearings, the edges of woods, water meadows and hilly areas with hedges, also in gardens.

Flight period: Mid-Mar to early Sep; two broods, but one at higher altitudes.

Behaviour: Commonly rests on the leaves of shrubs and trees; feeds on wet soil, carrion and tree sap, occasionally also at flowers; ♀ lays eggs singly on buds of the caterpillar's food plants.

Caterpillar: Short and rather stout, green or red-brown with a delicate white pattern, with fine hairs. Feeds mainly on holly and ivy, but also on certain other plants; consumes buds, flowers and fruits; attractive to ants, which feed on secretions from glands at the hind end. Chrysalis ochre-brown and spotted, usually attached to the underside of a leaf.

Hibernation: As a chrysalis.

2 Damon Blue *Agrodiaetus damon*

(Blues)

Description: Wingspan 3.3-4 cm. Upperside of ♂ (picture) silver-blue with a broad dark edge, ♀ entirely brown; underside of both sexes pale ochre-brown with a few black dots, hind wing with a characteristic white streak.

Distribution: Southern Europe, and at isolated localities in central Europe, to over 2000 m in mountains; in dry open grasslands, generally on limestone.

Flight period: Late June to early Oct; one brood.

Behaviour: Feeds on nectar, especially at thistles and Marjoram; eggs laid singly on dry seed capsules of the caterpillar's food plants.

Caterpillar: Yellowish green with dark and pale stripes, with dense hairs. Feeds on various species of sainfoin; always attended by ants. Chrysalis greenish- or yellowish-brown, smooth.

Hibernation: As an egg or young caterpillar.

3 Cranberry Blue *Vacciniina optilete*

(Blues)

Description: Wingspan 2.4-2.6 cm. Upperside of ♂ (picture) deep violet-blue with a black margin and white fringe; ♀ dark brown, overlaid with violet; underside whitish brown with rows of black spots, margin of hind wing with one or two red spots with shining metallic centres.

Distribution: Wet tundra of northern Europe, and in central Europe on high moors in the Alps and other mountain ranges (up to 2500 m).

Flight period: Late June to early Aug; one brood.

Behaviour: Similar to that of the Damon Blue, but eggs laid on the underside of leaves of the caterpillar's food plants.

Caterpillar: Woodlouse-shaped, green with yellowish side stripes, with velvety hairs. Feeds on Cranberry, Crowberry, Bilberry and Cross-leaved Heath. Chrysalis greenish, attached by a girdle to the underside of leaves.

Hibernation: As a caterpillar.

1

2

3

1 Large Skipper 🦋

(Skippers)

Ochlodes venatus

Description: Wingspan 3-3.5 cm. Upperside dark brown, with russet to orange spots and patches that are larger in ♂ (picture) than in ♀; ♂ also with a black strip of scent scales at middle of forewing; underside yellowish brown, tinged with olive, with an inconspicuous yellow pattern.

Distribution: Throughout Europe except for northern Scandinavia and Scotland, in mountains up to 2000 m; on grassy slopes, edges of woods and banks, and fallow land.

Flight period: Late May to early Sep; one brood, but two in the south.

Behaviour: With a hovering flight, usually close to the ground; unceasingly active in sunny weather, only resting briefly on leaves; regularly visits flowers; ♀ lays eggs singly on the upper surfaces of grass blades.

Caterpillar: Green with yellowish side stripes and a stout, black-brown, pale patterned head. Lives in a grass blade rolled to form a 'tent', on Tor Grass, Cocksfoot, Purple Moor-grass and other species of grass. Chrysalis slender, blackish, in a cocoon within the grass 'tent'.

Hibernation: As a fully grown caterpillar in a rolled-up leaf.

2 Small Skipper 🦋

(Skippers)

Thymelicus sylvestris

Description: Wingspan 2.6-3 cm. Upperside light russet-brown with a narrow black border and pale fringe; forewing of ♂ with a thin black line of scent scales; underside ochre-yellow, partly overlaid with grey-green.

Distribution: Central and southern Europe, up to 1800 m; in meadows, banks, and grassy flower-rich woodland edges and clearings.

Flight period: Late June to mid-Aug; one brood.

Behaviour: As for the Large Skipper, but eggs laid in the leaf sheath close to the node.

Caterpillar: Light green with a dark line on back and yellowish lines on sides, head dark green. Lives on Yorkshire Fog and other soft grasses, in a 'tent' of grass blades drawn together with silk thread. Chrysalis light green with a reddish sheath for the proboscis, in a loose cocoon within the tent.

Hibernation: As a caterpillar, in a closely woven, white, silk cocoon.

Similar species: The Essex Skipper 🦋 (*Thymelicus lineola*) has black tips to underside of antennae; distribution and life-cycle similar. The Lulworth Skipper 🦋 (*Thymelicus acteon*, small picture) is darker in colour; widespread in western Europe, in Britain confined to Dorset coast.

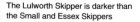

The Lulworth Skipper is darker than the Small and Essex Skippers

1

2

Chequered Skipper 🦋 *Carterocephalus palaemon*
(Skippers)

Description: Wingspan 2.4-3 cm. Upperside (picture 1) with yellow spots and patches on a dark brown ground-colour, underside (picture 2) pale ochre-yellow, hind wing with light spots.

Distribution: Throughout Europe to the far north, but absent from the Mediterranean, in Britain now confined to western Scotland, in mountains to over 1500 m; in scrubby meadows and grassy areas in open woodland.

Flight period: Late Apr to mid-July; one brood.

Behaviour: Sometimes in very large numbers where it occurs; a hovering flight, close to the ground; ♀ lays eggs singly on the blades of the caterpillar's food plants (grasses).

Caterpillar: Slender, green when young, becoming straw-yellow when hibernating. Feeds on False Brome, moor-grasses, Cocksfoot, Timothy Grass, Tor Grass and other grasses; spins grass blades together to form a tube-like shelter which it leaves only to feed, and in which it forms a whitish chrysalis with a pattern of brown stripes.

Hibernation: As a caterpillar, inside grass blades spun together with silk.

Silver-spotted Skipper 🦋 *Hesperia comma*
(Skippers)

Description: Wingspan 2.8-3.2 cm. Upperside golden-brown, forewing of ♂ with a black comma-like streak of scent scales divided by silver, which is absent from the altogether darker ♀ (small picture); underside (picture right) light olive-brown with small white patches.

Distribution: Throughout Europe, from coasts to over 2500 m; in unimproved meadows, dwarf-shrub heaths, woodland clearings, field banks and dunes.

Flight period: Late June to early Sep; one brood.

Behaviour: Hovering, erratic flight; a frequent flower visitor; eggs laid singly on grasses.

Caterpillar: Black-green with a stout shining head, virtually unhaired. Feeds on Perennial Ryegrass, Sheep's Fescue and other grass species; spins several blades of grass together to form a protective 'tent' in the centre of grass tufts. Chrysalis shining black, in a loose cocoon in the moss layer.

Hibernation: As an egg.

The ♀ of the Silver-spotted Skipper has single light spots on the wings.

1

2

3

1 # Dingy Skipper ♜ *Erynnis tages*
(Skippers)

Description: Wingspan 2.5-3 cm. Upperside dark brown with ill-defined light and dark spots, underside yellowish brown, with a row of fine whitish spots along outer margin of wings.

Distribution: Throughout Europe apart from northern Scandinavia, up to 2000 m in mountains; on meadows and heaths, the grassy edges of woods, and road verges.

Flight period: Early Apr to late Aug; two broods, but only one at higher altitudes and in the north.

Behaviour: Feeds at flowers on nectar; commonly rests on bare ground, with wings slanted backwards, roof-like; eggs laid on the upperside of leaves of the caterpillar's food plants.

Caterpillar: Rather stout, grey-green with a black-brown head. Feeds on Crown Vetch, Horseshoe Vetch and Bird's-foot Trefoil, where it spins leaves together to form a protective shelter, leaving it only to feed. Chrysalis greenish brown, in a loose cocoon in the moss layer.

Hibernation: As a fully grown caterpillar in its shelter.

2 # Grizzled Skipper ♜ *Pyrgus malvae*
(Skippers)

Description: Wingspan 2.2-2.6 cm. Upperside black-brown with contrasting white speckling, underside with lighter brown ground-colour.

Distribution: Throughout Europe except for the far north, in mountains up to 2000 m; in unimproved meadows, heaths, the edges of woods, roadside verges, field banks, especially on limestone.

Flight period: Early Apr to Aug; usually one brood.

Behaviour: A hovering flight, close to the ground; commonly suns itself on the ground with wings obliquely slanted; eggs laid singly on the leaf undersides of the caterpillar's food plants.

Caterpillar: Green to brown-green with a stout, dark brown head, with short bristly hairs. Feeds on various herbaceous plants such as species of cinquefoil, agrimony or Wild Strawberry; usually in a rolled-up leaf or in a 'tent' of several leaflets spun together. Chrysalis light brown, densely bristled, with rows of black spots, in a cocoon at the base of the food plant.

Hibernation: As a chrysalis, sometimes through two winters.

The caterpillar of the Grizzled Skipper feeds on Wild Strawberry.

1 # Olive Skipper
Pyrgus serratulae

(Skippers)

Description: Wingspan 2.4-2.8 cm. Upperside black-brown, suffused with grey, with an interrupted white fringe, forewing with small white splashes; underside olive-brown, with white patches.

Distribution: Central Europe and mountainous regions in southern Europe, up to 2500 m; in rather dry meadows and other moderately dry, sunny, open areas in hilly regions, usually on limestone.

Flight period: Mid-May to Sep; one brood.

Behaviour: Rapid hovering flight, usually just above the ground; visits flowers to feed on nectar, often spending the night on blooms; eggs laid on the underside of cinquefoil leaves.

Caterpillar: Green with a stout black head, after the third moult purple-red to black-brown, with short hairs. Feeds on various species of cinquefoil; rests in a shelter of several leaves spun together, leaving only to feed. Chrysalis light brown, with a black pattern and dense bristles, in a 'tent' of leaves in the moss layer.

Hibernation: As a half-grown caterpillar in a stout cocoon.

Note: Specimens from high in the Alps are distinctly smaller, with the white forewing splashes very reduced.

Similar species: The even more delicately marked Dusky Grizzled Skipper (*Pyrgus cacaliae*, picture 2) flies at high localities in the Alps, between 1600 m and 2500 m, from mid-June to Aug. Caterpillar feeds on Alpine Avens, Colt's-foot and Butterbur as well as on cinquefoils.

3 # Safflower Skipper
Pyrgus carthami

(Skippers)

Description: Wingspan 3-3.4 cm. Upperside with rectangular white spots on a dark grey-brown background, fringes banded light and dark.

Distribution: Central and southern Europe, up to 2200 m in mountains; in sunny localities with low vegetation in treeless and steppe-like countryside.

Flight period: Mid-May to early Sep; one brood.

Behaviour: Similar to that of the Olive Skipper.

Caterpillar: Green-grey with a stout black head, with whitish hairs. Feeds on Silverweed and other species of cinquefoil as well as various species of mallow. Chrysalis as in the Olive Skipper.

Hibernation: As a caterpillar.

1

2

3

1 Tufted Marbled Skipper *Carcharodus flocciferus*

(Skippers)

Description: Wingspan 2.8-3.4 cm. Very similar to the Mallow Skipper, but the white spots more distinct, even on hind wing, ♀ (picture right) overlaid with silver-grey, ♂ (small picture) with brown ground-colour; underside of hind wing with a pattern of radiating streaks.

Distribution: Southern and southern central Europe, in mountains up to 2000 m; like the Mallow Skipper, in warm dry habitats but also in damp meadows.

Flight period: Early June to Aug or Sep; two or three broods.

Behaviour: As for the Mallow Skipper.

Caterpillar: Rather stout, blue-grey with a black head, with white hairs. Feeds on various species of betony, horehound and woundwort; lives in a shelter of leaves drawn together with silk. Chrysalis brown with striking bluish dust, remaining in the larval shelter.

Hibernation: As a caterpillar, but occasionally as a chrysalis.

2 Mallow Skipper *Carcharodus alceae*

(Skippers)

Description: Wingspan 2.6-3 cm. Fore- and hind wings marbled with different shades of brown, forewing with short white cross-bands; underside similar, but more yellowish brown; hind-margin of hind wing with toothed appearance.

Distribution: Central and southern Europe, in mountains to over 1600 m; in warm dry steppe countryside, sunny river valleys, the edges of paths, and road and railway embankments.

Flight period: Early Apr to mid-Sep; two or three broods.

Behaviour: Flies singly; not confined to one place, and in favourable summers commonly migrates northwards; often rests on the ground, where it is best camouflaged; passes the night like a moth, with wings folded together like roof tiles; ♀ lays eggs singly on the upperside of leaves of the caterpillar's food plants.

Caterpillar: Reddish grey with very fine light dots, black head and yellow spots at neck, with dense hairs. Feeds on Marsh Mallow, Large-flowered Mallow, Musk Mallow and other species of mallow; remains within rolled-up leaves, leaving only to feed. Chrysalis slender, brown, blue-dusted, within the shelter of spun leaves.

Hibernation: As a fully grown caterpillar in a cocoon in the tube of leaves.

The ♂ of the Tufted Marbled Skipper is patterned with different shades of brown.

1 Humming-bird Hawk-moth 🦋

(Hawk-moths)   *Macroglossum stellatarum*

Description: Wingspan 4-5 cm. Forewing grey-brown with black transverse lines, hind wing orange to yellow; abdomen expanded and with elongated scales, resembling a bird's tail.

Distribution: Southern Europe, migrating every summer northwards into central Europe and Britain, sometimes to southern Scandinavia, in mountains as far as the limit of vegetation; usually on shrubby slopes, clearings and edges of woods, heaths, and gardens.

Flight period: Migrates northwards Apr-July, produces second brood Sep-Oct; in south up to four broods.

Behaviour: Flies by day, with a nimble hovering flight from flower to flower; feeds on nectar whilst hovering in the air like a humming bird; ♀ lays eggs singly on buds or flowers of the caterpillar's food plants.

Caterpillar: Green at first, becoming red-brown with fine white dots, white lines on back and sides, and a blue abdominal horn with a yellow tip; without hairs. Feeds on various species of bedstraw. Chrysalis in a loose silk cocoon on the ground.

Hibernation: As a chrysalis or adult moth, but does not usually survive the winter north of the Alps.

2 Broad-bordered Bee Hawk-moth 🦋

(Hawk-moths)   *Hemaris fuciformis*

Description: Wingspan 4-4.5 cm. Wings transparent except for a red-brown border; body wide, with ochre brown hairs; abdomen with a red-brown band, white flanks, and black tip.

Distribution: Throughout Europe, in mountains up to 2000 m; edges of woods and clearings, sunny riverside woods, and on mountain slopes.

Flight period: Early May to July, with one brood, or to Aug, with two broods.

Behaviour: Flies by day, with a jerky flight; visits many flowers, feeding on nectar whilst hovering; eggs laid singly on the underside of leaves of the caterpillar's food plants.

Caterpillar: Intense green with red-brown spots on sides and a brown abdominal horn, without hairs. Feeds on honeysuckle, more rarely on Snowberry. Chrysalis black-brown, in a silken cocoon just under the surface of the ground.

Hibernation: As a chrysalis.

Note: Its resemblance to a bee in appearance and behaviour (mimicry) protects it from enemies.

The caterpillar of the Humming-bird Hawk-moth feeding on Lady's Bedstraw.

1 # Eyed Hawk-moth 🦋 *Smerinthus ocellata*
(Hawk-moths)

Description: Wingspan 7-8.5 cm. Forewing extensively dappled grey-brown; hind wing dusky pink with a large blue-black eye-spot.
Distribution: Throughout Europe almost to the Arctic Circle, in mountains up to 2000 m; in open deciduous forests, water meadows and shrubby countryside, also in gardens and parks.
Flight period: Early May to Aug; usually one brood.
Behaviour: Only active at night; spends the day well camouflaged on tree bark; does not feed (proboscis stunted). When disturbed or alarmed by an enemy, it moves the forewings and flashes the 'eyes' on the hind wings; ♀ lays apple-green eggs singly or in pairs on leaves of the caterpillar's food plants.
Caterpillar: Bluish green, with a row of oblique yellowish stripes along sides, the latter continuing on to the slender bluish 'horn'. Feeds on various species of willow and sallow, also on poplars, fruit trees and other deciduous trees. Chrysalis shiny dark brown, just below the surface of the ground.
Hibernation: As a chrysalis.

2 # Spurge Hawk-moth (🦋) *Hyles euphorbiae*
(Hawk-moths)

Description: Wingspan 7-8.2 cm. Forewing pale brown, partly overlaid with pink and with large olive-green spots; hind wing with broad black-red-black bands.
Distribution: Central and southern Europe, a rare migrant to southern England, in mountains to over 1800 m; on sunny slopes and field banks.
Flight period: Early May to July with one brood, or to Sep with two broods.
Behaviour: Flies at dusk; feeds at flowers on nectar; ♀ lays eggs in small batches on leaves of spurge.
Caterpillar: With an unusually colourful and striking pattern of black, yellow and red; head, false legs, claspers and abdominal horn red; without hairs. Feeds on Cypress Spurge and other species of spurge. Chrysalis sand-coloured, in a loose cocoon just below the surface of the ground.
Hibernation: As a chrysalis, sometimes over several winters.

3 # Lime Hawk-moth 🦋 *Mimas tiliae*
(Hawk-moths)

Description: Wingspan 7-7.8 cm. Wings extensively dappled light and dark brown, suffused with pink and/or olive-green, colour and pattern very variable; outer wing-margins with jagged indentations.
Distribution: Throughout Europe, in mountains up to 1500 m; in deciduous and mixed woods, parks, old gardens.
Flight period: Late Apr to late July; one brood.
Behaviour: Flies only on warm nights; eggs laid singly or in pairs on the underside of leaves of the caterpillar's food plant.
Caterpillar: Green with oblique yellow stripes on sides, with fine yellowish-white dots, abdominal horn yellow, red and blue; without hairs. Feeds on lime, elm, alder and other deciduous trees. Chrysalis red- or black-brown, on or in the soil at the foot of the host tree.
Hibernation: As a chrysalis.

1 # Pine Hawk-moth 🦋 *Hyloicus pinastri*

(Hawk-moths)

Description: Wingspan 7.5-8 cm. Forewing grey-brown with blurred bands, delicately mottled, hind wing brown, fringes narrow and alternating dark brown and white.

Distribution: Throughout Europe, from lowlands up to 1600 m; in dry coniferous forests, especially in sandy pine forests.

Flight period: Early May to Aug; one brood.

Behaviour: Flies from early evening until late into the night; hovers from flower to flower whilst seeking food, preferring strongly scented flowers; rests by day on conifer trunks, where it is well camouflaged; ♀ lays eggs two or three at a time on needles on the caterpillar's host trees.

Caterpillar: Green at first, later increasingly reddish brown with black transverse and white longutudinal lines, a brown striped head, and a brown or black abdominal horn. Lives on pines or spruce, but only rarely on other conifers; feeds steadily on needles, even by day. Chrysalis black-brown, below the needle litter or in an earthen cocoon in the soil.

Hibernation: As a chrysalis.

2 # Willow-herb Hawk-moth

(Hawk-moths) *Proserpinus proserpina*

Description: Wingspan 4.5-5 cm. Forewing grey-brown with a broad dark cross-band, more or less overlaid with olive-green; hind wing dark yellow to orange, with a black-brown margin; outer wing margins very indented.

Distribution: Southern and southern-central Europe, up to 1500 m; on the warm and sunny margins of standing water, embankments of rivers, roads and railways, also on sandy soils.

Flight period: Early May to late June; one brood.

Behaviour: Flies at dusk, occasionally also by day; has a hovering flight, and can remain motionless in the air; feeds at flowers on nectar, especially on strongly scented blooms; eggs laid singly on leaves of the caterpillar's food plants.

Caterpillar: Grey-brown to dirty green, with black transverse streaks, abdominal 'horn' represented only by a tubercle. Feeds on Evening Primrose, Purple Loosestrife and various species of willow-herb; active at night. Chrysalis red-brown, in a small cell in the soil.

Hibernation: As a chrysalis.

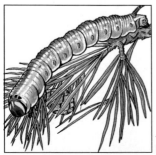

The caterpillar of the Pine Hawk-moth feeds on pine needles.

1   Death's Head Hawk-moth 🦋

(Hawk-moths)   *Acherontia atropos*

Description: Wingspan 11-13 cm. Forewing resembling tree bark, hind wing and abdomen patterned with ochre-yellow and black; upperside of thorax with a yellow design that resembles a skull.

Distribution: In Africa and southern Europe, migrating northwards every year across the Mediterranean and the Alps, small numbers reach the British Isles each year; up to 2000 m; prefers sheltered valleys, but also warm slopes in mountain ranges.

Flight period: Immigrants arrive from May to July, and the next brood from Aug to Oct (breeds in central Europe only at low altitudes).

Behaviour: Flies in late evening and at night; a rapid, jerky flight; feeds on nectar and flowing tree sap, and even enters bee hives occasionally to feed on honey; eggs laid singly on the underside of leaves of the caterpillar's food plants.

Caterpillar: Green to lemon-yellow, with diagonal blue to purple stripes on the sides; abdominal horn hanging down like a 'tail'; without hairs. Feeds mainly on potatoes, but also on other plants such as Deadly Nightshade, Privet or Thorn-apple; feeds at night; when disturbed produces a clicking sound and raises the front part of the body defensively; chrysalis shining black- or red-brown, buried up to 20 cm deep in the soil.

Hibernation: As a chrysalis or adult moth, but in central Europe does not survive the winter.

Note: When disturbed the adult can produce a strikingly loud squeaking sound.

2   Elephant Hawk-moth 🦋   *Deilephila elpenor*

(Hawk-moths)

Description: Wingspan 6-7.2 cm. Wings and body-hairs banded with rose-red and olive-green, base of hind wing black.

Distribution: Throughout Europe except for the far north, in mountains up to 1900 m; usually in rough areas, woods and on sloping banks, also in gardens.

Flight period: Mid-May to July, with one brood, or to Sep with two broods.

Behaviour: Active at dusk; feeds on nectar whilst hovering at flowers; eggs laid singly on leaves of the caterpillar's food plants.

Caterpillar: Brown and resembling bark, anterior part of body with striking

eye-spots and resembling a snake's head when it takes up a defensive pose (anterior part raised and stretched). Feeds on willow-herbs, bedstraw, fuchsia, grapevines and other plants; active at night. Chrysalis in leaf litter or directly on the ground.

Hibernation: As a chrysalis.

The caterpillar of the Elephant Hawk-moth feeds on Rosebay Willow-herb. In the defensive position it resembles a snake's head.

1 Scarlet Tiger 🦋   *Callimorpha dominula*

(Tigers)

Description: Wingspan 5-6 cm. Forewing black with larger and smaller white and yellow spots, hind wing red (rarely even yellow) with black spots.

Distribution: Throughout most of Europe, but mostly in isolated localities, northwards to central Scandinavia, in mountains up to 1500 m; in damp forest clearings, riverside woods, river banks.

Flight period: Late May to mid-Aug; one brood.

Behaviour: Flies by day, but also attracted to light at night; visits flowers to feed on nectar; eggs laid in small groups on the caterpillar's food plants.

Caterpillar: Black with broken yellowish-white bands on back and sides; with black hair-tufts on tiny warts. Feeds on a wide variety of plants, such as comfrey, stinging nettle, Bramble, Meadowsweet, Hemp Agrimony or dead-nettle; active by day, feeding even in bright sunlight; when disturbed, falls to the ground, rolls into a ball and feigns death. Chrysalis shining red-brown, in a thin cocoon among leaf litter on the ground.

Hibernation: As a young caterpillar.

2 Garden Tiger 🦋   *Arctia caja*

(Tigers)

Description: Wingspan 5-7 cm. ♀ distinctly larger than ♂. Forewing dark brown with a white, irregular, reticulate pattern, hind wing and abdomen orange with large black spots.

Distribution: Throughout Europe, from lowlands up to 1800 m; in open woods, shrubby areas, river plains, parks and gardens.

Flight period: Late June to Sep; one brood.

Behaviour: Flies at night and is attracted to light; does not feed (proboscis stunted); ♀ lays eggs in large batches on the underside of leaves of the caterpillar's food plants.

Caterpillar: Black-brown with dense tufts of long hairs that are red-brown on sides of body and are on small warts. Feeds on a wide variety of plants; behaviour as in the Scarlet Tiger. Chrysalis in a silken cocoon between plant stems on or close to the ground.

Hibernation: As a young caterpillar.

Similar species: The Cream-spot Tiger 🦋 (*Arctia villica*, picture 3) inhabits central and southern Europe, and has a black forewing with cream-coloured spots. It flies from late Apr, occasionally also by day.

The caterpillar of the Garden Tiger feeds on many herbaceous plants, such as sorrel and dock.

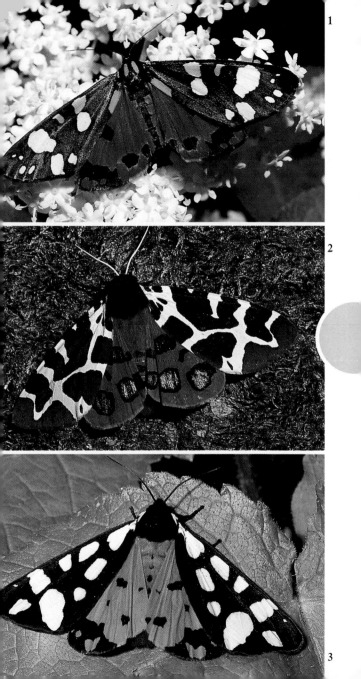

1 # White Ermine 🦋   *Spilosoma lubricipeda*
(Tigers)

Description: Wingspan 3.5-4 cm. A white moth with more or less numerous black dots on upperside of wings; thorax with strikingly long dense hairs; abdomen yellow with a row of black dots.

Distribution: Throughout Europe except for the Arctic region, in mountains up to 1600 m; on the edges of woods, shrubby countryside and fallow land, also in parks and gardens.

Flight period: Late Apr to late July; one brood; in warm regions, a second brood in Aug and Sep.

Behaviour: Flies at night, and frequently attracted to light; does not feed (proboscis stunted); rests by day on grasses or herbaceous plants; when disturbed, it falls to the ground, curves the abdomen as a danger signal, and feigns death; ♀ lays eggs in large batches on leaves of the caterpillar's food plant.

Caterpillar: Dark grey-brown with an orange-red stripe on back and black hair-tufts. Feeds on a wide variety of herbaceous plants; gregarious when young, but living singly later. Chrysalis red-brown, flattened, in a loose cocoon on or just above the ground.

Hibernation: As a chrysalis.

2 # Wood Tiger 🦋   *Parasemia plantaginis*
(Tigers)

Description: Wingspan 3.5-4 cm. Forewing black with a pattern of irregular whitish stripes, hind wing of ♂ (picture) yellow with black spots, more rarely white with black spots or almost entirely black, in ♀ always yellow with black spots.

Distribution: Throughout Europe, preferring hilly and mountainous country, up to 3000 m; in damp meadows, woodland clearings, moors.

Flight period: Late May to July, to Aug high in the Alps; one brood.

Behaviour: Flies by day, the ♂ in numbers when the sun is shining; ♀ very inactive and generally resting in the lowest layers of the vegetation.

Caterpillar: Black-brown with tufts of black and red-brown hairs. Feeds on small herbaceous plants such as Dandelion, plantain and sorrel. Chrysalis in a loose cocoon on the ground.

Hibernation: As a young caterpillar.

Further species: High in mountains, between 2000 m and 2600 m, the Northern Tiger (*Grammia quenselii*, small picture) is to be found: ♂ hovers on sunny days above alpine meadows whilst searching for ♀; caterpillar black-yellow with russet-red hairs, feeding on Dandelion, plantain, Wood Avens and other plants, hibernating through two winters.

The Northern Tiger's colour is perfectly adapted to the lichen covered rocks of its habitat.

1

2

1 Spotted Tiger　　　　　　　　　*Rhyparia purpurata*
(Tigers)

Description: Wingspan 4.5-6 cm. Forewing dark yellow with grey spots, hind wing purple-red with black spots.

Distribution: Central and southern Europe, with isolated localities north of the Alps; in mountains up to 1500 m; in damp meadows, fallow land, heaths.

Flight period: Early June to late July, one brood; south of the Alps also with a few second generation moths until Sep.

Behaviour: Active late at night, the ♂ occasionally flying in bright sunshine; rests by day on small plants, often on the underside of leaves.

Caterpillar: Dark grey with tufts of light grey hairs that are red-brown (occasionally even yellow) on back. Feeds on many herbaceous plants and low shrubs; often basks in the sun. Chrysalis shining dark brown, in a silken cocoon on the ground.

Hibernation: As a young caterpillar.

2 Jersey Tiger 🗒　　　　　　　　*Euplagia quadripunctaria*
(Tigers)

Description: Wingspan 5.5-6 cm. Forewing black with yellowish-white bands, hind wing brilliant red with black spots; abdomen orange with rows of black dots.

Distribution: Central and southern Europe including southern England, rarely above 1000 m; on warm dry slopes, fallow land, parks and gardens.

Flight period: Early July to early Sep, one brood; inactive during the hottest months in the south (aestivation).

Behaviour: Active by day; feeds on nectar at flowers, particularly on thistles; ♀ lays eggs in small batches on the edges of leaves of the caterpillar's food plants.

Caterpillar: Dark brown with broken orange and yellowish-white longitudinal stripes, with tufts of short brown hairs. Feeds on herbaceous plants such as willow-herb, dead-nettle or Stinging Nettle, and after hibernation on hazel, honeysuckle, Raspberry and Blackberry; feeds mainly at night, spending the day concealed beneath leaves. Chrysalis in a loose cocoon in leaf litter.

Hibernation: As a young caterpillar.

Further species: The Cinnabar Moth 🗒 (*Tyria jacobaeae*, small picture) flies in warm dry areas, especially by day; caterpillars with black and yellow rings, with few hairs, feeding on Ragwort, usually gregariously.

The intense red of the Cinnabar Moth is eye-catching even at dusk.

1

2

1 Nine-Spotted

Syntomis (Amata) phegea

(Tigers)

Description: Wingspan 3.3-4 cm. Wings blue-black with white spots; abdomen elongated, with a whitish to golden-yellow spot and 'girdle' on upperside.

Distribution: Central and southern Europe but absent from Spain, at isolated localities north of the Alps, up to 1500 m in mountains; on sunny, flower-rich slopes, edges of woods, quarries.

Flight period: Late May to mid-Aug; one brood.

Behaviour: Flies by day; feeds on nectar at flowers, especially at thyme and Lavender; ♀ lays eggs in batches on leaves of the caterpillar's food plants.

Caterpillar: Dark grey with small warts bearing tufts of short black hairs; head brown-red, with fine hairs. Feeds on Dandelion, plantain, sorrel, dock, dead-nettle and other herbaceous plants; gregarious when young, solitary later. Chrysalis within a cocoon on the ground.

Hibernation: As a young caterpillar in a communal 'nest'.

2 Emperor Moth 🦋

Pavonia pavonia

(Emperor Moths)

Description: Wingspan of ♂ 5-5.8 cm, of ♀ 6-8.5 cm. Forewing of ♂ (picture) grey-brown, hind wing ochre-yellow, in ♀ all wings whitish grey-brown, both sexes with a large eye-spot on each wing.

Distribution: Throughout Europe, in mountains up to the tree line at some 2000 m; in open woods, moors, heaths and rough areas.

Flight period: Late Mar to early June; one brood.

Behaviour: Only ♂ active by day, flying around erratically whilst searching for ♀; ♀ rests in low vegetation, releasing a special scent to attract ♂, and usually flies only at night; eggs laid in dense batches around twigs of the caterpillar's food plants.

Caterpillar: Black at first, grass-green when fully grown with black spots or transverse stripes on which there are orange-yellow bristly warts. Feeds on Blackberry, Raspberry, buckthorn, Ling, Bilberry, Meadowsweet and other plants; gregarious when young. Chrysalis stout, purplish brown, in a bottle-shaped cocoon spun across a fork in the food plant.

Hibernation: As a chrysalis, sometimes through two winters.

3 Great Peacock

Saturnia pyri

(Emperor Moths)

Description: Wingspan 11-14 cm. Wing grey-brown, each one with a light outer margin and a large 'eye'.

Distribution: Southern and southeast Europe, northwards to the southern Alps and Lower Austria, to over 1600 m; along the edges of woods, tree-covered slopes, orchards.

Flight period: Early Apr to early June; one brood.

Behaviour: Flies at night; otherwise like the Emperor Moth.

Caterpillar: Black at first, yellow-green when fully grown, with blue warts bearing tufts of black bristles. Feeds on fruit trees and other deciduous trees. Chrysalis in a brown pear-shaped cocoon lodged in the fork of a twig or branch.

Hibernation: As a chrysalis, sometimes through two winters.

Note: The largest moth in Europe.

1

2

3

1 Oak Eggar 🔲   *Lasiocampa quercus*
(Eggars)

Description: Wingspan of ♂ 5-6.5 cm, of ♀ 6-8.5 cm. ♂ (picture) reddish- to dark brown, each wing with a yellow cross-band fading out towards outer margin, forewing with a white central dot; ♀ usually ochre-brown with a less contrasting pattern.

Distribution: Throughout Europe, to over 2000 m; in open woods, high moors, hedgerows and heaths.

Flight period: Mid-May to Sep; one brood.

Behaviour: ♂ flies on sunny days, with a rapid zigzag flight, searching for ♀; ♀ flies at night, resting by day among low plants; eggs dropped singly amongst foliage whilst in flight.

Caterpillar: Black-brown, with a pattern of white streaks on sides, with yellow-brown hairs. Feeds on Hawthorn, oak, birch, heather, Raspberry, Bilberry, and various deciduous trees. Chrysalis stout, black-brown, in a coarsely woven brown cocoon in the grass.

Hibernation: As a caterpillar, in cooler regions through another one or two winters as a chrysalis.

2 Pine-tree Lappet   *Dendrolimus pini*
(Eggars)

Description: Wingspan of ♂ 5-6 cm, of ♀ 6.5-7.5 cm. Very variable, forewing dappled with yellowish grey through red-brown to black-brown, with a white central spot, hind wing uniformly brown; ♀ (picture) generally light grey-brown, pattern weaker.

Distribution: Throughout Europe, in mountains to over 1600 m; in coniferous forests, usually of pine.

Flight period: Early June to mid-Aug; one brood.

Behaviour: Active mainly at night, ♂ sometimes also flying by day; ♀ disinclined to fly; eggs laid singly or in small batches on pine needles.

Caterpillar: Grey-brown with a row of dark lozenge-shapes on back and two blue bands behind head, with red-brown hairs. Feeds on pines, rarely also spruce. Chrysalis black-brown with reddish hairs, in a dense cocoon.

Hibernation: As a half-grown caterpillar, rolled up in the ground litter.

3 Lappet 🔲   *Gastropacha quercifolia*
(Eggars)

Description: Wingspan of ♂ 5.2-5.5 cm, of ♀ 7-8.5 cm. Body and wings reddish brown, often with a purplish metallic sheen; wings with jagged edges.

Distribution: Throughout Europe except northern Scandinavia, but not above 900 m; in open deciduous forests, hedgerows, gardens and orchards.

Flight period: Mid-June to Aug; one brood, but two broods in the south.

Behaviour: Flies at night, resting by day on twigs with wings folded over the back, looking deceptively like a dry leaf; ♀ lays eggs singly or in small batches on the underside of leaves of the caterpillar's food plants.

Caterpillar: Grey- to reddish-brown with two blue bands behind head, with brown hairs. Feeds on Sloe, sallow, Buckthorn, fruit trees and other deciduous trees. Chrysalis within a spindle-shaped cocoon against a twig.

Hibernation: As a half-grown caterpillar on a twig.

1 **Vapourer Moth** 🗒   *Orgyia antiqua*

(Tussocks)

Description: Wingspan of ♂ 2.8-3.2 cm. ♂ (picture) orange-brown, forewing with dark shadows and transverse lines as well as a white spot; ♀ with only tiny vestiges of wings, abdomen stout and with yellowish-brown fur.

Distribution: Throughout Europe, in mountains up to 1600 m; in deciduous and mixed woods, parks and gardens.

Flight period: Mid-May to Oct; two to three broods.

Behaviour: ♂ flies by day, searching for ♀ with a frenzied zigzag flight; ♀ unable to fly, resting on her empty cocoon and releasing a special scent to attract ♂; eggs commonly laid on the old cocoon.

Caterpillar: Dark grey with tufts of long pale hairs on red warts, with four brush-like tufts of yellow hairs on back. Feeds on sallow, beech, oak, Sloe, Bilberry, blackberry and many other deciduous trees; chrysalis in a fine cocoon on tree trunks, thick plant stalks, lattice fences etc.

Hibernation: As an egg.

Note: The caterpillar's hairs may be irritant to human skin.

2 **Gipsy Moth** (🗒)   *Lymantria dispar*

(Tussocks)

Description: Wingspan of ♂ 3.5-4 cm, of ♀ 4.5-5.5 cm. ♂ (picture) grey-brown, marbled with delicate zigzag lines, ♀ whitish with fine brown zigzag lines.

Distribution: Throughout Europe apart from northern Scandinavia, up to 1200 m in mountains; in deciduous and mixed forests, parks and orchards.

Flight period: Early July to early Sep; one brood.

Behaviour: Active by day; does not feed (proboscis stunted); ♂ searches for ♀ with a rapid zigzag flight; ♀ flies very rarely, generally resting on tree trunks and giving off a special attractant from its scent glands; lays hundreds of eggs in a single batch on the bark of trees; hairs from the ♀ abdomen remain stuck to the eggs and give the egg batch a fungal appearance.

Caterpillar: Pale ochre-yellow and black, with long tufts of brown hairs on red and blue-black warts. Feeds on the leaves of oak, poplar, fruit trees and other deciduous trees, but also on conifers. Chrysalis red-brown, haired, in a loose cocoon between leaves.

Hibernation: As an egg.

Note: Extinct in Britain where it now occurs only as an occasional vagrant.

The caterpillar of the Gipsy Moth commonly lives on oaks.

1   # Black Arches 🦋   *Lymantria monacha*

(Tussocks)

Description: Wingspan of ♂ 3.6-4.2 cm, of ♀ 4.5-5 cm. Forewing with black spots and zigzag lines on a white background, hind wing beige with a border of black marks; ♀ (picture right) with a more contrasting pattern than ♂.

Distribution: Throughout temperate Europe, up to 1600 m in mountains; especially in coniferous forests, but also in deciduous woods.

Flight period: Early July to Sep; one brood.

Behaviour: Flies late in the evening and at night; ♀ seldom flies, attracting ♂ with a special scent; eggs laid in small batches in crevices of tree bark, generally on lower part of trunk.

Caterpillar: With a dark and light grey pattern, with tufts of short grey hairs. Feeds at night especially on pine and spruce, but also on other coniferous and deciduous trees. Chrysalis on a tree-trunk, within a thin cocoon.

Hibernation: As an egg.

2   # Brown-tail Moth 🦋   *Euproctis chrysorrhoea*

(Tussocks)

Description: Wingspan 3-4 cm. Wing pure white; tip of abdomen with yellow-brown hairs, developed in ♀ as a dense tuft (♂ shown in picture).

Distribution: Throughout Europe, northwards to central Scandinavia, up to 1400 m in mountains; in open deciduous woods, parks and orchards.

Flight period: Early June to Aug; one brood.

Behaviour: Similar to that of the Black Arches; but ♀ lays eggs in a single batch on the underside of leaves of the caterpillar's food plants and covers the batch with numerous abdominal hairs.

Caterpillar: Black with orange-red spots on back and tufts of grey-brown highly irritant hairs. Feeds on a wide variety of deciduous trees; young caterpillars construct a fixed communal silken nest which they leave only to feed. Chrysalis black-brown with pale hairs, in a small cocoon singly among leaves.

Hibernation: As a young caterpillar in the communal 'tent'.

3   # Pale Tussock 🦋   *Calliteara pudibunda*

(Tussocks)

Description: Wingspan of ♂ 4.2-4.8 cm, of ♀ 5.6-6.2 cm. Ground-colour beige, with brownish shadows, forewing of ♂ (picture, right) with a broad brown band, of ♀ with only thin transverse lines.

Distribution: Throughout temperate Europe, in mountains up to 1600 m; in deciduous forests, parks and gardens.

Flight period: Mid-Apr to late July; one brood, in some areas with a second brood in autumn.

Behaviour: Flies at night, resting by day on tree trunks or among low vegetation; ♀ lays eggs in batches on tree trunks.

Caterpillar: Generally yellow or pale green, even grey, with black transverse bands, with long hairs, with four stout tufts of yellowish hairs on back and a long tuft of red hairs at hind end. Feeds on birch, oak, elm, lime and other deciduous trees. Chrysalis black-brown with yellowish hairs, on the ground and enclosed in a cocoon mixed with the caterpillar's hairs.

Hibernation: As a chrysalis.

1 | Six-spot Burnet 🦋 | *Zygaena filipendulae*
(Burnets)

Description: Wingspan 3-4 cm. Forewing black, shining metallic blue-green, with six carmine-red spots; hind wing carmine-red with a black edge.
Distribution: Throughout Europe, to over 2000 m in mountains; in unimproved meadows, fallow land, also on the edges of woods.
Flight period: Mid-June to Sep, south of the Alps even in late May; one brood.
Behaviour: Active by day; fluttering flight; feeds at flowers on nectar; falls to the ground when disturbed and feigns death; commonly forms 'dormitory' colonies in the evening on flowers or plant stems; wings folded roof-like over the back when at rest; ♀ lays eggs in batches on the upperside of leaves of the caterpillar's food plants.
Caterpillar: Short and stout, yellow-green with rows of black and yellow spots; head black; with short hairs. Feeds on Bird's-foot Trefoil, more rarely on Scorpion Vetch and species of sainfoin. Chrysalis within a yellowish, boat-shaped, parchment-like cocoon attached to plant stems.
Hibernation: As a caterpillar, sometimes over two winters.
Note: The red spots act as a warning colour that alerts potential enemies that the moths are distasteful.

2 | Eastern Burnet | *Zygaena carniolica*
(Burnets)

Description: Wingspan 2.8-3.5 cm. Forewing black, with a metallic blue-green sheen, with six shining-red, white-edged spots; hind wing red.
Distribution: In southern Europe and at isolated localities in central Europe, up to 1500 m; in sunny dry meadows, slopes, edges of woods; often very numerous in the areas where it occurs.
Flight period: Mid-June to late Aug; one brood.
Behaviour: Similar to that of the Six-spot Burnet.
Caterpillar: Pale blue-green with longitudinal white lines and a pattern of black and yellow dots, with whitish hairs. Feeds on Bird's-foot Trefoil and species of sainfoin. Chrysalis in a yellowish oval cocoon attached to sections of plant just above the ground.
Hibernation: As a caterpillar.

Similar species: The Variable Burnet (*Zygaena ephialtes*, small picture) is locally common in warm, dry, unimproved meadows or heaths in July and Aug; the blue-black forewing has five or six white, red or yellow spots.

The colour of the wing spots is highly variable in the Variable Burnet.

1 **Rosy Underwing** (♑)   *Catocala electa*
(Owlets)

Description: Wingspan 6.5-7.5 cm. Forewing grey-brown with a pattern resembling bark; hind wing with crimson and black bands.

Distribution: Central and southern Europe, a very rare migrant to Britain; up to 1400 m; in riverside woods, river valleys, damp parks and gardens.

Flight period: Mid-June to early Oct; one brood.

Behaviour: Active at night, resting by day on tree trunks with the brightly coloured hind wings concealed beneath the camouflaging forewings; ♀ lays eggs singly in crevices in the bark.

Caterpillar: Ochre-yellow with small black dots and small yellow warts, without hairs. On sallow, feeding at night on the leaves. Chrysalis slender, between leaves or in crevices of the bark.

Hibernation: As an egg.

Similar species: The Red Underwing ♑ (*Catocala nupta*) is slightly darker in colour. Widespread in Europe, including Britain.

2 **Clifden Nonpareil** ♑   *Catocala fraxini*
(Owlets)

Description: Wingspan 8-9.5 cm. Forewing grey-brown with a mottled pattern resembling bark, hind wing black-brown with a white fringe and light blue transverse band.

Distribution: Throughout Europe apart from the extreme south, scarce in Britain, up to 1600 m in mountains; in mixed deciduous forests, water meadows, more rarely in parks and mature gardens.

Flight period: Late July to Nov; one brood.

Behaviour: Active at night, resting by day on tree trunks where it is well camouflaged; feeds on ripe fruits and flowing sap; timid, flying rapidly away when disturbed; ♀ lays eggs singly in crevices in bark.

Caterpillar: Slender, grey with a dappled brown pattern, without hairs. Lives mainly on willow and poplar, more rarely on ash and other deciduous trees; feeds at night; rests by day pressed against a twig and is difficult to see. Chrysalis dark brown with blue dusting, in a loose cocoon among dry leaves on the ground.

Hibernation: As an egg.

3 **Yellow Riband**   *Ephesia fulminea*
(Owlets)

Description: Wingspan 5-6 cm. Forewing grey-brown, with a coarse zigzag marbled pattern; hind wing with intense yellow and black-brown bands.

Distribution: Central and southern Europe, not over 1200 m; on the sunny edges of woods, shrubby slopes, hedgerows, parks, and also orchards.

Flight period: Late July to late Aug; one brood.

Behaviour: Similar to that of the Clifden Nonpareil.

Caterpillar: Slender, grey or brown, with an uneven warty surface which gives it the appearance of a twig. Feeds mainly on Sloe, plum, and more rarely on oak or hawthorn; found mainly in the lower part of the tree. Chrysalis slender, in a loose cocoon.

Hibernation: As an egg.

1

2

3

1 Herald 🦋 *Scoliopteryx libatrix*

(Owlets)

Description: Wingspan 4-4.5 cm. Ground-colour light brown; forewing with reddish areas, outer margin jagged.

Distribution: Throughout Europe though less widespread in the south, up to 2000 m in mountains; in damp forests, water meadows, moors, parks, gardens.

Flight period: Early June to Aug, with a second brood from Sep to following May.

Behaviour: Active at night; feeds at flowers, but also at ripe fruit; ♀ lays eggs singly or in small batches on twigs and leaves of the caterpillar's food plants.

Caterpillar: Slender, grass-green with yellow side stripes, without hairs. Feeds on the leaves of willows and poplars; simply falls when disturbed. Chrysalis elongate, matt black, in a white cocoon between a 'tent' of leaves.

Hibernation: As an adult moth, in hollow tree trunks, caves and other sheltered corners, even in buildings.

2 Angle Shades 🦋 *Phlogophora meticulosa*

(Owlets)

Description: Wingspan 4.4-5 cm. Forewing olive-brown, overlaid with pink, with a dark V-shaped pattern; hind wing yellowish brown with dark lines.

Distribution: The Mediterranean area, but migrates northwards every year to central Europe and occasionally into southern Scandinavia, both immigrant and resident in Britain, up to 2000 m in mountains; around hedgerows, agricultural areas, rough land and gardens.

Flight period: Every month of the year, but mainly May to Oct.

Behaviour: Active at night; feeds at flowers on nectar; eggs laid singly or in small batches on leaves of the caterpillar's food plants.

Caterpillar: Stout, greenish or brown, with a pattern of lighter and darker lines, without hairs. Feeds at night on a wide variety of plants, such as stinging nettle, bindweed, dock, Blackberry or sallow, remaining concealed by day. Chrysalis slender, red-brown, in a loose cocoon just underground.

Hibernation: As an adult moth or as a caterpillar.

3 Merveille du Jour 🦋 *Dichonia aprilina*

(Owlets)

Description: Wingspan 4-4.6 cm. Ground-colour light blue-green to dark moss-green, with a pattern of black spots and zigzags and lighter whitish patches.

Distribution: Throughout temperate Europe, rarely above 1000 m; in dry deciduous and mixed forests, water meadows, parks and old gardens.

Flight period: Late Aug to mid-Nov; one brood.

Behaviour: Active at night; feeds at flowers on nectar; ♀ lays eggs singly or in small batches on oak twigs or in crevices in the bark.

Caterpillar: Stout, reddish brown to grey-green with a black and white pattern, with short bristles. Feeds on oak, occasionally on other deciduous trees; feeds at first in the centre of the buds, but later lives in the open on the leaves; active at night, concealed by day in bark crevices. Chrysalis stout, brown, in a large cocoon in the soil among the roots.

Hibernation: As an egg.

1

2

3

1 ## Silver Y 🦋 *Autographa gamma*

(Owlets)

Description: Wingspan 3.5–4.2 cm. Forewing brown to grey, patterned like bark, with a white mark in the middle that resembles the Greek letter gamma (γ); hind wing brown, white-edged; front part of body with three erect tufts of hairs.

Distribution: Southern Europe, migrating every year into other parts of Europe, to over 2000 m in mountains; in fields, meadows, water meadows, and gardens.

Flight period: Migrants arrive after early Apr, with two to three broods until Nov; some individuals return south in autumn.

Behaviour: Flies by day and at night; feeds at flowers on nectar; eggs laid singly or in small batches on the caterpillar's food plants.

Caterpillar: Green with whitish or yellowish longitudinal stripes, with sparse bristles. Feeds usually at night, on numerous wild and cultivated plants such as clover, pea or cabbage. Chrysalis brown-black, in a transparent cocoon between leaves.

Hibernation: As a caterpillar, but only in the south.

Note: Occasionally the caterpillars become crop or garden pests.

Similar species: Another day-flying Owlet, the grey but brightly patterned Mother Shipton 🦋 (*Callistege mi*, picture 2), is found in damp and dry unimproved meadows from late Apr to Sep. The caterpillars are very slender, light brown, with longitudinal lines, and feed mainly on species of clover.

3 ## Green Silver-lines 🦋 *Pseudoips fagana*

(Owlets)

Description: Wingspan 3.2–4 cm. Forewing lime-green with darker and lighter diagonal bands; hind wing yellowish in ♂, white in ♀.

Distribution: Northern, central and parts of southern Europe, up to 1500 m; in deciduous and mixed forests, hedgerows, parks.

Flight period: Early May to late July, one brood; in the south, to late Aug with two broods.

Behaviour: Active at night; rests by day on fern fronds or on other low plants; can produce a crackling noise; eggs laid singly on leaves or twigs.

Caterpillar: Stout, green with thin yellow lines on sides, without hairs.

Feeds mainly on oak, beech, birch and hazel, but also on other deciduous trees. Chrysalis in a boat-shaped, paper-like cocoon which is spun on to a leaf or a crevice in bark.

Hibernation: As a chrysalis.

The caterpillar of the Mother Shipton feeds commonly on Red Clover.

1

2

3

1 Mottled Umber 🗒   *Erannis defoliaria*

(Geometers)

Description: Wingspan 3.5-4 cm. Forewing of ♂ (picture right) light grey-brown to dark red-brown with wavy cross-bands, hind wing creamy; ♀ (small picture) without wings, body light grey with black spots.

Distribution: Throughout Europe, up to 1400 m in mountains; on the edges of woods, hedgerows, parks and gardens.

Flight period: Late Sep to Dec; one brood.

Behaviour: The ♂ flies at dusk and at night, and is attracted to the ♀ by special scents; prior to mating, ♀ climbs up a tree trunk where ♂ finds her; eggs laid singly on leaf buds.

Caterpillar: Pale to dark russet-brown with a band of yellow spots on sides, without hairs. Lives on beech, oak, birch, fruit trees and other deciduous trees; moves in a characteristic 'looper' manner; when disturbed, lowers itself to the ground on a silken thread. Chrysalis in an earthen chamber under the ground.

Hibernation: As an egg.

Note: Caterpillars can be fruit tree pests as they devour buds, flowers, leaves and fruit.

2 Netted Carpet 🗒   *Eustroma reticulatum*

(Geometers)

Description: Wingspan 2.2-2.8 cm. Forewing black-brown with a white latticed pattern, hind wing grey.

Distribution: Throughout temperate Europe, but not above 1100 m; in damp woods, shaded valleys and riverbanks.

Flight period: Early June to mid-Aug; one brood.

Behaviour: Active at night; feeds at flowers on nectar; rests by day on leaves with wings outspread, often alongside paths where it sometimes takes briefly to the air; ♀ lays eggs singly on the underside of leaves of the caterpillar's food plant.

Caterpillar: Pale green with red-brown and white longitudinal lines, without hairs. Feeds only on Touch-me-not Balsam, consuming first the leaves, then the flowers and ripening seeds. Chrysalis ochre-brown, shining, in a strong cocoon among the leaf litter.

Hibernation: As a chrysalis.

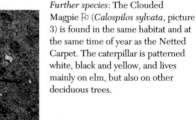

Further species: The Clouded Magpie 🗒 (*Calospilos sylvata*, picture 3) is found in the same habitat and at the same time of year as the Netted Carpet. The caterpillar is patterned white, black and yellow, and lives mainly on elm, but also on other deciduous trees.

The ♀ of the Mottled Umber has no wings.

1

2

3

1 ## Speckled Yellow 🦋   *Pseudopanthera macularia*
(Geometers)

Description: Wingspan 2.6-3 cm. Wings golden-yellow with blackish spots;
ground-colour varying from orange to whitish yellow, becoming noticeably
paler with age.
Distribution: Throughout Europe except for Arctic regions, up to 1900 m;
in open woodlands and warm shrubby areas.
Flight period: Late Apr to mid-July; one brood.
Behaviour: Flies in bright sunshine; feeds at flowers on nectar, commonly
in large numbers, otherwise resting on grasses or herbs; eggs laid on leaves
of the caterpillar's food plants.
Caterpillar: Slender, green, with dark back and white stripes on sides,
without hairs. Feeds on Wood Sage, dead-nettle, woundwort, mint and
related plants. Chrysalis on the ground in a cocoon mixed with soil or moss.
Hibernation: As a chrysalis.

2 ## Brimstone Moth 🦋   *Opisthograptis luteolata*
(Geometers)

Description: Wingspan 2.8-4.2 cm. Wings lemon-yellow, on fore-margin of
forewing with a white, dark-edged spot and several pale red-brown spots.
Distribution: Throughout Europe, to over 1500 m; in open deciduous and
mixed forests, hedgerows, parks and gardens.
Flight period: Early May to mid-Aug, one brood; in climatically favourable
areas from Apr to Oct, with two broods.
Behaviour: Flies mainly at night, but occasionally by day; when disturbed
opens and closes its wings and then folds them above its head; eggs laid on
leaves of the caterpillar's food plants.
Caterpillar: Green or grey-brown, back warty. Feeds on hawthorn, Sloe
and other deciduous trees. Chrysalis in a dense cocoon on the ground.
Hibernation: As a chrysalis, sometimes even as a caterpillar.
Further species: Another brightly coloured Geometer, the Orange Moth 🦋
(*Angerona prunaria*, picture 3) is also found in similar habitats. Its
ground-colour very variable, orange to pale yellow, more or less densely
streaked with grey, and even dark brown specimens occur. Flies mainly at
night, but also in the afternoon. Rests on the underside of leaves with wings
spread out. Caterpillar (small picture) mottled grey-brown, feeding on
various deciduous trees; overwinters.

The caterpillar of the Orange Moth
perfectly resembles a twig.

Colourful caterpillars

Lappet

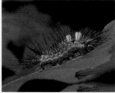
Pale Tussock

Orange Moth

Narrow-bordered Burnet

Camberwell Beauty

Spotted Tiger

Magpie Moth

Peacock

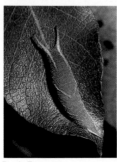
Purple Emperor

Sycamore Moth

Death's Head Hawk-m

Small Tortoiseshell   Swallowtail

Spurge Hawk-moth

Garden Tiger

Spotted Fritillary   Vapourer Moth

Pine-tree Lappet   Speckled Wood

Introduction to butterflies and moths

Often regarded as 'flying jewels' or 'nature's gems', butterflies and moths are without doubt some of the best-known and best-loved insects on earth. But in general our interest is directed towards only the adult insects, whilst there is much less concern for the earlier stages. Indeed, many people have a horror of caterpillars; some caterpillars are vigorously combated as garden or orchard pests, whilst others are simply not noticed. But without caterpillars there can be no butterflies and no moths. We should therefore take an interest in *all* the life stages of these fascinating and beautiful creatures.

What are butterflies and moths?

Butterflies and moths are insects. With over 140,000 species known and described so far, they inhabit almost every region of the earth. Like all insects, they possess an external skeleton composed of chitin and sclerotin, which are tough and astonishingly resistant materials. So that movement is possible within this 'armour', the skeleton is actually composed of many individual plates which are connected by membranes.

The body is divided into three sections: the **head**, containing the sensory organs, the **thorax**, to which legs and wings are attached, and the **abdomen**.

On the **head** the most striking elements are the two enormous **eyes**. They are so-called compound eyes, which consist of many hundred to several thousand individual hexagonal eye-facets. Through them the butterfly obtains a mosaic-like image of its surroundings. In addition, a number of species, especially the moths, have some additional simple eyes near the top of the head.

The feelers, which are usually known as **antennae**, are very different in form (see drawings on the inside of the front cover). They are sensory organs for the perception of sound waves and vibrations and, most importantly, of smells. The more complicated the structure of the antennae, i.e. the larger their surface area, the better they function as sensory organs.

In day-flying species there is a group of sensory bristles near the base of the antennae known as Jordan's organ, which may enable the insect to measure its speed of flight.

In addition to the eyes and antennae, there is a further striking structure on the head: the long **proboscis**. When it is not in use, this flexible, sheath-like, sucking tube is carried rolled up tightly beneath the head. When unrolled and extended it is so long in most species that nectar can be reached even in very deep and very narrow blooms. In some species, for example certain Hawk-moths, the proboscis is stunted and non-functional so that feeding only takes place in the caterpillar stage.

The **thorax** (chest section) consists of three segments that are firmly bonded together. To each of them is attached a pair of segmented legs. The **legs** are thin and not particularly suited for walking, but there are hooked claws on the last segment which make them effective for gripping. This region of the leg also has numerous sensory cells by means of which the butterfly locates food sources and, when laying eggs, the correct food plant for its caterpillars.

The two pairs of **wings** are attached to the middle and hind thoracic segments. Butterfly and moth wings are remarkably delicate and yet astonishingly stable structures. A network of fine tubes or veins gives the membrane its required strength. These tubes are filled with blood, and also contain nerves and air-tubes (tracheae). To the specialist, the precise pattern of the wing-veins is an important feature for the classification of the species and also for the exact identification of any adult insect.

For the layman who wishes to identify butterflies and moths, it is generally not necessary to look further than the characteristic patterns and colours of the wings. The marvellous colours are the product of millions of scales which cover the wing surface like tiles on a roof and which contain the various coloured pigments. Sometimes, however, the special structure of the scales refracts the light and produces a metallic shine or another fantastic reflective effect. Like all the other surfaces on the butterfly's body, the scales are covered with a fine film of wax which repels water and makes the insect 'weatherproof' to a certain extent. Also on the wings, especially in males, there are often special scales, the so-called scent scales, which are important for each sex in locating a partner. In some species the scales may be absent in places, and the transparent wing-membrane is then visible.

A major function of the **abdomen** is reproduction. In addition to the stomach and the 'heart' (a tubular pump muscle that circulates the yellowish blood that flows freely through the hollow spaces of the body), it contains the large and complicated reproductive organs. The external sexual organs are very diverse in form and are used by specialists as an important criterion for the identification of various species. At the tip of the abdomen, especially in the females of many moths, there are scent glands that disperse a secretion capable of attracting males over long distances.

Sun worshippers and night owls

The original and very simplified division of the thousands of species of butterfly and moth into two groups, large species and small species ('Macrolepidoptera' and 'Microlepidoptera') is now very much out of date, though still in general use as a purely practical tool. Students of classification ('systematics') are much more concerned with trying to analyse the evolutionary and family relationships of the species. Nevertheless, since time immemorial, the large species have been divided into butterflies (day flyers) and moths (night flyers). This division was based primarily on the time of flight activity but many exceptions are known, butterflies that fly at dusk or even at night and moths that are active during daylight hours. A species can be recognised as a butterfly or a moth by certain external features:

Butterflies have slender thread-like antennae with the tips thickened into knobs or spindles. When at rest the wings are closed together vertically above the body (except in some Skippers).

In Europe, the butterflies include as families the Swallowtails; the Whites and Yellows; the Browns, Aristocrats and Fritillaries; the Blues, Coppers and Hairstreaks; and the Skippers.

Moths, on the other hand, have antennae that are very varied in form. They may be bristle-like, toothed, feathered, comb-like, or covered with tufts of bristles. Males usually have distinctly larger and more elaborately structured antennae than females, since they have to detect at some considerable distance the subtle scents given off by females that are ready to mate. When at rest moths usually have the wings folded roof-like or flat over the body. In this way the fore-wings lie mainly or entirely over the hind-wings. The hind-wings are frequently different in colour or have a very contrasting pattern, and are only visible in flight or when the moth flashes them to deter a potential enemy or intruder.

The moths include the Hawk-moths; Silk Moths; Burnets; Tigers and Ermines; Tussocks; Eggars; Owlets; Geometers and many others.

Camouflage, mimicry and warning colours

Butterflies and moths have many enemies. If this were not the case, their great fertility would rapidly lead to a population explosion, their caterpillars would strip the land bare, and the basis of their own existence would thereby be destroyed. Eggs and caterpillars, as well as the adults themselves, are eaten by many enemies such as predaceous insects, spiders and birds.

To protect themselves from their enemies, butterflies and moths have developed various strategies. Many have developed colours and patterns on their wings that match perfectly the background on which they usually rest. Irregularly concave or jagged wing-margins blur their outlines and break up the typical butterfly silhouette. They merge imperceptibly into their surroundings. Moths in particular, which rest during daylight hours, are the true masters of camouflage. The inside back cover of this book shows some examples of this.

But it is not only the adults that develop a perfect camouflage – caterpillars and chrysalises may do so as well. It is particularly important for the chrysalis, which is considered by many birds to be a delicacy and is also quite incapable of escaping from predators. Caterpillars may even change colour in the course of their development – when they moult or because, for example, they may change food plant or the food plant itself may gradually wither.

In their colour, shape or behaviour, certain adults and caterpillars may imitate objects in their environment which are of no interest to predators, such as dry leaves, broken twigs, thorns, fragments of bark, or even bird droppings. Biologists call this kind of deception **crypsis**.

In addition to this, there are butterflies which have developed **mimicry**, a no less sophisticated kind of defence against enemies. Instead of making itself inconspicuous, as in the other system, the animal here grabs the attention because of its distinctive colour or pattern. Its tactic is to mimic a poisonous, distasteful or reactive creature which has a striking display of warning colours. Predators that have a disagreeable experience with such an insect learn to recognise the warning colours and prudently avoid them thereafter. Meanwhile, harmless and tasty butterflies that mimic the warning colours of distasteful insects deceive their potential predators into believing that they too are distasteful, and are left in peace. There are moths that mimic bumble bees, wasps or even hornets.

Other species display their garish colours with good reason. Burnet moths, for example, have poisonous substances in their blood. Their warning black and red or black and yellow colours are unmistakable, and any bird that has sampled a Burnet as prey will avoid having such a distasteful moth in its beak for a second time. Poisonous caterpillars also use warning colours. For example, the yellow and black rings of the caterpillar of the Cinnabar moth advertise its unpalatability.

A number of adult butterflies and moths have also developed a means for startling an enemy, and any slight hesitation or retreat by the confused attacker is then used for a rapid escape. The most effective shock is delivered by a contrasting pattern of eye-spots. Such eye-spots are generally concealed when at rest and are suddenly displayed when the insect is disturbed or threatened. The Peacock butterfly, for example, will spread its wings wide to display the eye-spots on the uppersides, whilst the Eyed Hawk-moth will rapidly move the fore-wings so as to display the pair of eye-spots concealed on the hind-wings.

Feeding

Butterflies and moths do not just provide a meal for other creatures; they must also feed themselves. Most of them do indeed do so, but there are some that do not feed as adults because their mouth-parts have degenerated. Such butterflies and moths live entirely on the fat reserves that they have accumulated during the caterpillar stage. In general their life span is extremely short.

Most butterflies and moths have a well-developed proboscis (sucking tube) with which they are able to imbibe liquid food. Most of them feed on plant fluids, primarily nectar from flowers but also running tree sap or even the juice from overripe fruits. Many of them like to feed on the very sugary exudations from plant lice ('honeydew'). Others prefer to feed on the liquids from mammal excrement or from carrion. The Death's Head Hawk-moth is known to love honey, and adults enter bee hives to obtain it. Some species are attracted to human sweat. Many species imbibe water from rain puddles and wet patches of soil, obtaining at the same time minerals dissolved in the water.

Reproduction

Special scents (pheromones) play a decisive role in enabling male and female butterflies and moths to locate each other. Females produce these pheromones in scent glands situated at the hind end of the body and are able to attract males over long distances. On the other hand, male pheromones are produced in the abdomen, the legs or, in the majority of cases, on the wings, but are only effective over short distances. Their function is to induce a female to copulate at the conclusion of courtship. But butterflies in particular also orientate themselves visually, that is to say they recognise a potential mate by the wing colour and pattern. Males of some species, particularly the Browns, are markedly territorial in their behaviour. They rest on some vantage point with a good view, and await passing females whom they immediately accost. If another male flies by, it is vigorously attacked and driven off. Various species have extensive and complex courtship flights prior to mating.

Copulation may last for hours, or even for several days with moths, and the partners remain with the tips of their abdomens connected. The genital organs are anchored so firmly together that a butterfly can even fly whilst copulating and can carry his partner.

A variable period elapses after mating before the female begins to lay eggs. Eggs are generally attached directly to the food plant by means of a sticky waterproof secretion, and according to the species may be laid in one batch or arranged tidily in a group or in a single row. Some females place their eggs at particular places in small batches or singly, while others lay them close to the food plant or simply drop them over suitable areas whilst in flight. Each female lays at least a few dozen eggs, but some lay several thousand. Egg laying can extend over several weeks in species that lay eggs singly in special situations. Examples of the variety of form found in eggs and egg-batches are given inside the front cover of this book.

The caterpillar (larva)

After a period of development, which varies greatly in length but is only partly dependent on the ambient temperature, the tiny caterpillar is fully formed inside the egg and chews its way out through the egg shell. From now on its motto is: eat, eat, and keep on eating. The sole purpose of the caterpillar's existence is to grow and to store up reserves of energy for the subsequent transformation into an adult. After eating the egg shell and the remains of the yolk, it turns to the food plant. Its appetite and consequent growth are enormous. For example, the caterpillar of the Swallowtail butterfly increases its weight a thousand-fold within two weeks – a record in the animal kingdom. The skin of a caterpillar does not stretch indefinitely, and before long it becomes too small. Beneath the old skin, a new one begins to form, larger and arranged in folds at first. Regulated by hormones, the caterpillar stops feeding one to three days before moulting and remains motionless. Then it bursts through the old skin behind the neck and casts it off backwards. The old skin is frequently consumed. In many cases the caterpillar changes in appearance with each moult, which increases still further the enormous diversity of caterpillar form and ornamentation. Caterpillars exist with almost every conceivable colour and pattern, bare, with short bristles or with soft hairs, covered with large and small warts or with dangerous-looking spines. However, the basic structure of the body is always the same.

The **head** is a robust, spherical capsule. It does not have compound eyes like the adult butterfly or moth, but has some simple eyes, and in addition a pair of tiny antennae and – indispensable for the caterpillar – a pair of powerful jaws modified for chewing.

Each of the three **thoracic segments** has a pair of short segmented legs. The segments of the abdomen have pairs of sucker-like 'false legs' (or 'prolegs') on the underside which have rows or circles of tiny hooks. Most species of caterpillar have four pairs of these false legs, and at the hind end a pair of so-called claspers. The number of false legs varies from group to group within the moths. For example, 'looper' caterpillars (Geometers) have the first three pairs missing, which has given rise to the characteristic 'looping' movement of these caterpillars.

The caterpillar's **internal organs** are fundamentally similar to the adult in terms of structure, though much simpler. Most of the space in the caterpillar body is taken up by the digestive organs and the fat body which later provides an energy reserve for the adult butterfly or moth. All caterpillars have a pair of silk glands in the abdomen, though these vary greatly in their development. They are most massively developed in the Silkmoth family: the product of the silk glands in silkworm caterpillars is the basis for the finest silks.

The miraculous transformation

Like the ugly duckling and the swan, each caterpillar that lives long enough and eats enough will one day transform into a butterfly or moth. This does not happen overnight, and in fact there is a special resting stage between caterpillar and adult: the **chrysalis** or **pupa**. The caterpillar's last moult reveals the chrysalis which at first has a soft outer skin that hardens into a fixed, more or less immovable chitinous armour. Many caterpillars prepare a protective silk cocoon around themselves within which they pupate. This may be a strongly woven case, as in the Silkmoths, or a loose web spun on to leaves or twigs, as in many Skipper butterflies. Many caterpillars pupate without any protective shell. According to their mode of attachment they can be classified into three types, which are also illustrated on the inside of the front cover:

Hanging chrysalises are suspended head-down from a leaf, twig or any other suitable object. They are firmly attached by a kind of hook at the tip of the abdomen.

Girdle-and-pad chrysalises stand the right way up. They are attached at the base by hooks at the tip of the abdomen, and held in position by a central girdle spun from silk and attached to the pupation site on a plant stem or other support.

Ground chrysalises either lie freely on the surface of the ground, between stones, beneath leaves of the herb layer, at the base of grass tufts, or are concealed at varying depths in the humus layer or the soil.

According to the species and the prevailing climatic conditions, the pupal stage may last from a few days to several years. During this time, the miraculous transformation from earth-bound caterpillar to winged adult takes place within the shell of the chrysalis. Emergence of the adult may take a few seconds or several minutes. The freshly emerged adult clambers up to a raised spot whilst the limp, soft and tightly folded wings gradually become functional. It pumps air and blood through the wing-veins. After about ten minutes the wings have expanded, and a few hours later they have hardened sufficiently for the butterfly to take its first flight.

Surviving the winter

Butterflies and moths have solved the problem of surviving the winter in many different ways. The most usual strategy is to find a sheltered situation and to enter a state of dormancy until conditions improve. This process, called hibernation, is adopted by many different animals. A similar process is undergone by some insects during the hottest and driest part of the summer and this is called aestivation.

Many adult butterflies and moths hibernate, some of them even choosing to spend the winter in unheated buildings, particularly in garden sheds and other outhouses. If there is a warm sunny spell during the winter months, some butterflies (e.g. Small Tortoiseshells) will become active and it is not unusual to see them flying on unseasonably warm days in January and February. Many hibernate in the caterpillar stage although again some may become active and start to feed again on mild winter days. Other butterflies and moths overwinter as eggs or chrysalises. It is interesting that many overwintering eggs contain fully developed caterpillars which are ready to hatch at the first signs of spring. Similarly many chrysalises overwinter with fully formed adults concealed within.

In southern parts of Europe, where winter temperatures are not so low, many butterflies and moths remain active in one stage or other throughout the year or adopt different overwintering strategies from their cousins in the north.

Threats and conservation

Over the last few years a lamentable trend has become increasingly obvious: fewer and fewer butterflies can be seen flitting over the meadows and fields of our countryside, and fewer and fewer are visiting the flowers in our gardens. Of the 59 native species of British butterflies, at least 50% have seriously decreased in abundance and range of distribution. Since the mid-nineteenth century, four species have become extinct and a number of other species are now considered to be under more or less serious threat of extinction. What is responsible for the disappearance of our butterflies and moths?

Butterflies and moths need flowers

They do not need just any flowers, but very particular ones. Most butterflies and moths have highly specific ecological requirements and do not just need flowers as a source of nectar but require particular flowers, grasses or trees as sources of food for their caterpillars. The majority of caterpillars are very choosy where their food plants are concerned, and they will starve rather than feed on a 'wrong' plant. Most of the grasses and herbs that serve as food plants grow on unimproved soils that are poor in nitrogen. Our modern intensive agricultural use of meadows has been brought about by an 'improvement' of the soils by the application of artificial fertilisers and liquid manure. The result has been that plants that avoid nitrogenous soils have disappeared, and with them the butterflies and moths that are dependent on them. The caterpillars that can survive on the tough and robust grasses of fertilised meadows disappear when regular cutting takes place, ending up in the stomachs of cattle or in haystacks.

Woodland species have not fared much better. Modern forestry invests almost exclusively in large dark plantations of conifers in which there is no place for the flower- and herb-rich clearings or for the broad shrubby margins that are so favoured by butterflies.

In addition to the loss of suitable habitats, the widespread use of poisonous chemicals that are sprayed indiscriminately for plant protection in forests, farms and gardens poses another threat to butterflies and moths. It may be that the insecticides themselves give caterpillars and adults the finishing stroke, or that the herbicides used against 'weeds' are depriving caterpillars of their food plants – the upshot is that one way or another the poisons released by man into the environment are destroying the populations of butterflies and moths.

What each of us can do

It is not just for the big businesses of forestry and agriculture to make some allowance for butterflies and moths – conservation begins at home, in the garden. If we turn a monotonous lawn into a wild-flower meadow, if we tolerate weeds and especially Stinging Nettles in one corner of the garden, if we plant native flowering shrubs instead of exotic ornamental shrubs, then we have already done something for our butterflies and moths. It goes without saying that every nature-lover should entirely give up the use of poisonous sprays.

A 'butterfly garden' does not have to be overgrown and unattractive. All we need do is remember that blooms with a long narrow corolla tube are usually preferred by both butterflies and moths. Well-known garden flowers that give pleasure to us and to butterflies and moths include Marjoram, Honeysuckle, Tobacco Plant, Ice Plant, Honesty, Valerian, Marigolds, Wallflower, Thyme, Lavender, Ragged Robin, Phlox, Aster, Alyssum, Rosebay Willow-herb and, of course, Buddleia which is still popularly known as the 'butterfly bush'.

With only a little effort, space can certainly be found for some of the main caterpillar food plants. Important plants include Stinging Nettle, Thistles, Cuckooflower, Wild Carrot, Sorrel and Bird's-foot Trefoil, as well as a variety of grasses and shrubs such as Buckthorn, Sloe and various Sallows and Willows.

Another way to help butterflies and moths is to join a local or national conservation society. In the British Isles there is Butterfly Conservation (formerly the British Butterfly Conservation Society). There are also many active local and county naturalists trusts and conservation societies that make a valuable contribution towards the welfare of wildlife in general. It is important to remember that butterflies and moths cannot be conserved in isolation and that it is essential to protect their environment if they are to survive. For this reason, taking part in any well-planned conservation scheme will indirectly benefit butterflies and moths by saving natural environments.

National conservation organisations:

British Naturalists' Association, 48 Russell Way, Higham Ferrers, Northamptonshire NN9 8EJ

British Trust for Conservation Volunteers, 36 St. Mary's Street, Wallingford, Oxfordshire OX10 0EU

Butterfly Conservation, PO Box 222, Dedham, Colchester, Essex CO7 6EY

The RSNC Wildlife Trusts Partnership, The Green, Whitham Park, Waterside South, Lincoln LN5 7JR

Butterfly centres:

London Butterfly House, Syon Park, Brentford, Middlesex RW8 8JF, tel. (0181) 5600378

Stratford-upon-Avon Butterfly Farm, Tramway Walk, Stratford-upon-Avon, Warwickshire CV37 7LS, tel. (01789) 299288

Edinburgh Butterfly and Insect World, Melville Garden Centre, Lasswade, Edinburgh, Midlothian EH18 1AZ, tel. (0131) 663 4932

Worldwide Butterflies Limited, Compton House, Nr Sherbourne, Dorset DT9 4QN, tel. (01935) 74608

INDEX